Paul Burns

REVISION PLUS

AQA

GCSE English Literature

Revisim Companion

Contents

Contents

4 Course Overview

Grammar and Language

6 Quality of Written Communication (QWC)
7 QWC: Punctuation, Spelling and Grammar
9 Literary Terms
11 Planning and Checking
12 Referring to the Text

Modern Texts

13 Unit 1: Exploring Modern Texts
14 Modern Texts: Ideas, Themes and Issues
17 Modern Texts: Characters
21 Modern Texts: Settings
24 Modern Texts: Language and Techniques
28 Modern Texts Section A: Exam Tips
29 Modern Texts: Exam Practice
30 Developing Your Answer
32 Modern Texts: Exploring Cultures
36 Exam Practice
38 Developing Your Answer

Poetry

40 Poetry
42 Reading a Poem
43 Poetry: Ideas, Themes and Issues
45 Poetry: Character and Voice
47 Poetry: Form and Structure
49 Poetry: Language
52 Comparing Poems
54 Exam Tips
55 Exam Practice
56 Developing Your Answer
58 Unseen Poetry
60 Unseen Poetry: Exam Practice
62 Unseen Poetry: Planning Your Answer
63 Unseen Poetry: Exam Practice
64 Poetry: Approaching Unit 5

Shakespeare and the English Literary Heritage

65 Shakespeare and the English Literary Heritage
66 Shakespeare: Ideas, Themes and Issues
68 Shakespeare: Characters
70 Shakespeare: Settings
73 Shakespeare: Genre
74 Shakespeare: Form

75 Shakespeare: Language
77 The English Literary Heritage
78 The ELH: Ideas, Themes and Issues
80 The ELH: Characters
82 The ELH: Settings
84 The ELH: Genre and Form
85 The ELH: Language and Techniques
86 Exam Tips
87 Exam Practice: Section A
88 Developing Your Answer
90 Exam Practice: Section B
92 Developing Your Answer
94 Approaching Unit 3

95 List of Authors
96 Index

Course Overview

This book is suitable for use by students studying AQA GCSE English Literature.

How the Course is Assessed

The GCSE English Literature course is assessed by…
- two exams (75% of the total mark)
- controlled assessment (25% of the total mark).

There are **two** assessment routes available. You will find more information about these on page 5.

Controlled Assessment Explained

Controlled assessment has replaced coursework. Controlled assessment involves completing a task within a set number of hours.

AQA will provide a range of tasks for you to choose from. Your teacher will help you choose the most suitable task for you.

The purpose of controlled assessment is to see how well you can bring all your skills and knowledge together to respond to a text.

You must produce individual work under controlled conditions, i.e. under the formal supervision of a teacher. Your teacher can review your work and give you general feedback. However, all the work must be your own.

You will be given time to plan and prepare for the controlled assessment. You may take brief notes in with you, but not drafts of essays or detailed plans. Notes must be submitted for moderation. You must also keep a record of all the resources used during the planning phase and submit this record with your final piece.

You can use **clean** copies of the relevant texts during the formal assessment.

How Controlled Assessment is Marked
Your teacher will mark your work using guidelines from the AQA exam board. A moderator at the exam board will review these marks to ensure that they are fair.

About this Revision Guide

Whilst this book might quote or make reference to some of the set texts on the AQA GCSE English Literature specification, it does not provide a close reading or detailed analysis of these texts.

Instead, it recaps all the key skills that you need in order to read, understand and analyse texts so that you can come up with your own original ideas. This book covers the skills needed to read and analyse the following types of text:
- Modern prose and drama
- Texts from different cultures
- Poetry
- Shakespeare
- Prose from the English Literary Heritage

The skills covered are universal so they will help you in your exams and controlled assessment, regardless of which assessment route you choose.

The following books, published by *Letts Educational and Lonsdale*, are guides to the most popular set texts on the AQA GCSE English Literature specification:
- AQA Anthology Companion
- *Of Mice and Men* Text Guide
- *An Inspector Calls* Text Guide
- *To Kill a Mockingbird* Text Guide
- *Lord of the Flies* Text Guide
- *Macbeth* Text Guide
- *Romeo and Juliet* Text Guide

Course Overview

The course is divided into 'units'. There are five units altogether, but each student will only take **three**.

All students will take two exams and one controlled assessment (three units in total).

All students will take the exam on **Exploring Modern Texts**, which is worth 40% of the total marks.

You will all be assessed on both **poetry** and **Shakespeare and the English Literary Heritage**, but your teacher will choose which of these subjects you will do in class (controlled assessment) and which you do in an examination. The one that you do in the exam will be worth 35% of your total marks and the controlled assessment will be worth 25%.

The way the assessments are organised is shown below:

Unit 1: Exploring Modern Texts			
External Examination	40% of the total GCSE marks	1hr 30mins	60 marks
Section A: Modern Prose or Drama	20% of the total GCSE marks	45 mins	30 marks
Section B: Exploring Cultures	20% of the total GCSE marks	45 mins	30 marks

PLUS

EITHER

Unit 2: Poetry Across Time		
External Examination 35% of the total GCSE marks	1hr 15mins	54 marks
Section A: Poetry Cluster from the Anthology 23% of the total GCSE marks	45 mins	36 marks
Section B: Responding to an unseen poem 12% of the total GCSE marks	30 mins	18 marks

Unit 3: The Significance of Shakespeare and the English Literary Heritage		
Controlled Assessment 25% of the total GCSE marks	3–4 hours	40 marks
N.B. The times given are the amount of time allowed to produce a written response.		

OR

Unit 4: Approaching Shakespeare and the English Literary Heritage		
External Examination 35% of the total GCSE marks	1hr 15mins	54 marks
Section A: Shakespeare 20% of the total GCSE marks	45 mins	30 marks
Section B: Prose from the English Literary Heritage 15% of the total GCSE marks	30 mins	24 marks

Unit 5: Exploring Poetry		
Controlled Assessment 25% of the total GCSE marks	3–4 hours	40 marks
N.B. The times given are the amount of time allowed to produce a written response.		

Quality of Written Communication (QWC)

The quality of your written communication is assessed in all your units. The examiners want to see that you can express yourself clearly in Standard English.

This means that you must…

- make sure that your writing is legible
- organise your essays clearly and coherently
- use specialised vocabulary when needed, e.g. literary terms
- make sure that your spelling and punctuation are correct so that your meaning is clear
- use a form and style of writing (usually a formal style) that is appropriate for the task.

Organising Your Essays: Structure and Paragraphs

When you write an answer in an exam or controlled assessment, it is important that you structure it well. This means using clear, linked paragraphs, and developing a logical answer through your paragraphs.

Using paragraphs means you do not end up with a solid block of text, and it allows you to present your ideas in an organised way so that your points are easier to follow.

You should begin a new paragraph every time you start to write about something new. Usually, a paragraph starts with a 'topic sentence', which shows the reader that you are starting a new idea.

The best way to show that you are starting a new paragraph is to **indent.** Alternatively, you can leave a line between paragraphs, which is more usual in typed or printed work. For example:

> By using these images the poet expresses a sense of loss, and how his life has been changed forever.
>   This theme is present in both poems…

Or

> By using these images the poet expresses a sense of loss, and how his life has been changed forever.
>
> This theme is present in both poems…

Linking Paragraphs

Connectives are words and phrases that are used to link clauses, sentences or paragraphs. They help your writing to flow.

This is a list of some connectives that you might want to use when writing your answers.

- However…
- Consequently…
- Although…
- In addition…
- In conclusion…
- Therefore…
- Similarly…
- On the other hand…
- In contrast…

Opening and Closing Paragraphs

Your opening or introductory paragraph tells the reader what you are writing about. You might need to make it clear which texts you are writing about, especially if the question names one text and asks you to compare it to another. You should also answer the question briefly.

Here is an example of an introductory paragraph answering the question: 'Compare the ways in which childhood is presented in *Brendon Gallacher* and one other poem'.

> In both *Brendon Gallacher* and *Checking Out Me History* the poets look back on incidents from their childhoods. However, they choose different aspects of childhood and their memories reflect very different experiences. While Jackie Kay writes about her imaginary friend and what he meant to her, John Agard writes about the education he was given and how it shaped his feelings about himself and his background.

Your final paragraph should bring together the main ideas in your essay, summarising your points and trying to give a final, personal answer to the question. For example:

> Both these poems are very personal, telling us something about how the poets' childhood experiences shaped their lives and their sense of their own identity. However, the two poets use language and form in very different ways. Both the mood of the poems and the subject matter suggest they feel very differently when they look back on their lives although both seem to have come to terms with their backgrounds.

QWC: Punctuation, Spelling and Grammar

Correct use of punctuation and grammar is very important in order to convey clear meaning through a piece of writing. The following information is provided to help you when you are writing your answers in the English Literature exam (and in your other exams). Read the information through and make sure you understand it. You will be expected to use punctuation and grammar correctly in your written answers.

Full Stops (.)

Full stops separate sentences. Without them, writing does not make sense.

Commas (,)

A comma can be used to join two sentences into one, but it must be followed by a connecting word such as 'while', 'yet' or 'but', for example…
- He is bitter and spiteful, but he loves his family.

Commas are used to mark off parts of a sentence that give extra information, but are not necessary for the sentence to make sense, for example…
- Alice, his granddaughter, could be seen as selfish. The highlighted phrase and commas could be taken out and the sentence would still make sense.

Commas are also used to list items, for example…
- The old man is described as old-fashioned, bitter, stubborn and lonely.

Question Marks (?)

Question marks come at the end of questions, for example…
- Could the old woman be envious of the younger generation? ✓
- He asked if the old woman could be envious of the younger generation? ✗

Colons (:)

Colons are used before an example or explanation, for example…
- The poet uses onomatopoeia to describe the water: it 'trickles'.

Colons also appear before a list, for example…
- The poet has used many language techniques: alliteration, assonance and personification.

The part before the colon must be a complete sentence, but the part after it does not need to be.

Semi-colons (;)

Semi-colons are used to show that two clauses are closely related, for example…
- In *The Clown Punk,* childhood is portrayed through the adult's eyes; in *Brendon Gallacher*, it is portrayed through the child's eyes.

The parts before and after the semi-colon must be complete sentences.

Apostrophes (')

Apostrophes are used to show omission or contraction (usually in speech or in informal writing). The apostrophe replaces the missing letter(s), for example…
- He didn't want anything to change. (didn't = did not)
- He's finished his work but she's still doing hers. (he's = he has, she's = she is)

Apostrophes are also used to show possession. If the owner is singular (or plural but does not end in 's', e.g. sheep, men, children), add an apostrophe and an 's' to the word that indicates the owner, for example…
- The boy's grandfather. (i.e. the grandfather of the boy.)
- The girl's shoes. (i.e. the shoes of the girl.)
- The children's games. (i.e. the games of the children.)

If there is more than one owner (plural) and the word indicating the owners ends in 's', simply add an apostrophe at the end, for example…
- The boys' grandfather. (i.e. the grandfather of the boys.)
- The girls' shoes. (i.e. the shoes of the girls.)

Confusing Words

The following words are often used incorrectly. Make sure you know the correct way to use each one.

Done / did, and seen / saw

He did it	✓	He saw it	✓
He has done it	✓	He has seen it	✓
He done it	✗	He seen it	✗

Could, would, should, ought to, might, may, can, will
These are modal verbs. They are never followed by 'of'; they are followed by 'have', for example…
- She should have looked after her family. ✓
- She should of looked after her family. ✗

QWC: Punctuation, Spelling and Grammar

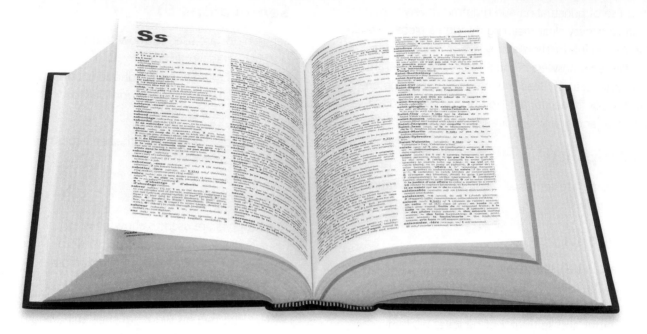

It is important that you spell and use words correctly in your answers in the exam. The following list contains words which are frequently misused. It will help you if you read through these words and learn the correct ways to spell and use them.

Accept   – to receive: 'he accepts the man's apology'.

Except   – apart from: 'they were all playing, except the girl'.

Its   – belonging to it: 'the eagle spread its wings'.

It's   – short for 'it is' (the apostrophe shows that the 'i' is missing): 'it's a sad poem'.

No   – opposite of 'yes': 'no, I don't like it'.

Know / knew   – being aware of something: 'he didn't know the girl knew about it'.

New   – opposite of old: 'it's a new story'.

Passed   – a verb: 'I passed all my GCSEs'.

Past   – a noun indicating a previous time: 'the story is set in the past'. (Also used in phrases such as 'he went past' or 'they are past their best'.)

Practice   – a noun: 'exam practice can be very helpful'.

Practise   – a verb: 'if you practise writing answers, you should do well in the exam'. (The same rule applies to advice / advise and licence / license.)

There   – in that place: 'he is there'. (Also used in phrases such as 'there is', 'there are', etc.)

Their   – belonging to them: 'they left their house'.

They're   – 'they are' (the apostrophe shows that the 'a' is missing): 'they're not happy anymore'.

Too   – excessively: 'the girl is too selfish'.

Two   – the number: 'he saw two flowers'.

To   – towards: 'he went to school'. ('To' is also part of the infinitive of a verb: 'to do', 'to think', etc.)

Where   – a place: 'where is it?'.

Wear   – used with clothes, etc.: 'she had to wear a coat'.

We're   – 'we are' (the apostrophe shows that the 'a' is missing): 'we're not sure'.

Were   – past tense of the verb 'to be': 'they were walking to the lake'.

Whether   – if: 'it is not clear whether it refers to the girl or to her mother'.

Weather   – the sun, wind, rain, etc.: 'the weather often reflects the characters' moods'.

Whose   – belonging to whom: 'whose book is it?'.

Who's   – 'who is' or 'who has' (the apostrophe shows that the 'i' or 'ha' is missing): 'who's that boy?', 'who's dropped that book?'.

Literary Terms

This is a list of terms that you will find useful when writing about literature. You have probably already used most of them in class when discussing the language and techniques that writers use in their work.

The terms are mentioned throughout this revision guide, so it will help you if you read through them before you start revising your texts. You can also refer back to these pages as you work your way through the book.

Adjectives: describe nouns and add detail, e.g. great, wonderful, yellow.

Adverbs: describe verbs (how the action is done). They usually end in 'ly', e.g. carefully, easily, quickly.

Alliteration: repetition of a sound at the beginning of words, e.g. 'river rushing rapidly'.

Ambiguity: the effect of a word or phrase that has more than one possible meaning (i.e. it is ambiguous).

Antagonist: someone who is opposed to the protagonist.

Aside: a line or two addressed to the audience by a character in a play.

Assonance: repetition of a vowel sound within words, e.g. 'how now brown cow', in order to convey a mood or feeling.

Colloquial language: informal language; the sort of language used in conversation; may include dialect words or phrases.

Connotation: a meaning that is suggested by the use of a word or phrase because of what is associated with it, e.g. red might indicate danger.

Contrast: a strong difference between two things.

Dialect: words or phrases particular to a region or area.

Dialogue: conversation, especially in a play.

Diction: the kind of words and phrases used, e.g. formal diction, violent diction, technical diction.

Enjambment: when a clause or sentence runs from one line of poetry to another, i.e. not stopping at the end of the line.

Exclamations: show anger, shock, horror, surprise and joy, e.g. 'We won!'

Genre: a specific type of writing, with its own conventions, e.g. detective story, romance, science fiction.

Hyperbole: exaggeration.

Imagery: 'painting a picture' in words, using descriptive language, metaphors or similes.

Imperatives: Commands or instructions, e.g. 'Don't do that!' or 'fry for ten minutes'.

Irony and sarcasm: the use of words to imply the opposite of their meaning. Sarcasm is a crude, obvious form of irony.

Juxtaposition: putting words or phrases (often contrasting) next to each other.

Metaphor: an image created by referring to something as something else, e.g. 'an **army** of nettles'.

Metre: the formal arrangement of a poem's rhythm, e.g. iambic pentameter.

Narrative: a story or an account of something.

Narrator: the person telling the story.

Onomatopoeia: a word that sounds like what it describes, e.g. splash, clang, click.

Oxymoron: two contradictory words placed together, e.g. 'cold fire', 'bitter sweet'.

Paradox: a statement that is contradictory or seems to be nonsensical, but is true, e.g. 'to gain peace, they went to war'.

Pathetic fallacy: when the surroundings (e.g. the weather) reflect the mood of a character.

Persona: a 'voice' or character adopted by a writer writing in the first person.

Personification: writing about an object or animal or idea as if it were a person, giving it human qualities, e.g. 'the wind whispered', 'Time will not wait for us'.

Protagonist: the main character.

Questions (interrogatives): show that the writer wants the reader to think about something or that the writer is thinking about it.

Repetition: when words, phrases, sentences or structures are repeated.

Literary Terms

Rhetorical question: a question which does not require an answer; used to make the listener think about an issue.

Rhythm: the beat of the writing, especially in poetry – fast or slow, regular or irregular.

Simile: a direct comparison of one thing to another, using the words 'as', 'like' or 'than', e.g. 'as big **as** a house', **'like** an angry lion', 'faster **than** a speeding bullet'.

Soliloquy: a speech addressed to the audience by a character in a play, telling the audience what he / she really thinks.

Standard English: the conventional use of words and grammar in the English language; used in formal writing.

Structure: how a text or story is organised and arranged.

Stanza: A division in a poem; the equivalent of a paragraph in prose.

Superlatives: words that express the best of something. They usually end in 'est' or have 'most' before them, e.g. 'happiest', 'biggest', 'most beautiful'.

Symbols and symbolism: a symbol is an object that represents an idea or feeling, e.g. a dove symbolises peace.

Tone: the overall feeling or attitude of the writing, e.g. formal, informal, sad, playful, angry, ironic.

Helpful Hint

It is useful to be able to use these terms with confidence, but remember that you should always explain the **effect** a technique has on the reader (you).

Planning and Checking

When you take a **controlled assessment** you will write your answer in a 'production' session. However, you will have seen the question before this assessment session. You will also have been given a chance to plan your answer in detail and may even have produced a practice essay. But, you are not allowed to take plans or drafts into the controlled assessment, so when taking your assessment you may still want to spend a bit of time making a plan, and it is very important to check your work.

In the **examinations** you will be seeing the questions for the first time. For each section of each exam you take, you should spend about five minutes planning your answer. At the end of the exam you should spend a few minutes checking your work.

The Importance of Planning

It is very important and helpful to plan your answers. A plan reminds you to structure your work properly – in paragraphs – and helps you to produce an answer that is clear, logical and flows well.

When you have chosen which question you are going to answer, read it through a few times so that you know exactly what you are being asked to do. Pay particular attention to the bullet points: you will lose marks if you do not cover all the bullet points. Underline key words.

If the question allows you to choose one of the texts you are answering on (as in Unit 2 Section A), choose it quickly but carefully. It should be a text you know well.
If the text, or an extract from it, is given to you (as in Unit 1 Section B and Unit 2 Section B), read it and underline or highlight any phrases you might want to refer to or quote.

Note down any thoughts you have and then try to put them in the order in which you will discuss them in your answer. You might do this by…
- using a spider diagram
- listing your ideas in columns and then numbering them
- planning it in the right order straightaway.

The Importance of Checking

Checking your work is just as important as planning it. Try to leave a few minutes at the end of the exam to read over your answers.
- Check that you have written in paragraphs. If you have forgotten to do this, indicate clearly where you should have started new paragraphs.
- Check that you have covered everything you wanted to cover.
- Check that the words you have used put across your points as you intended.
- Check your spelling and punctuation. It is easy to make mistakes when you are under pressure.

Helpful Hints

Make sure you label the plan as such, so that the examiner knows it is not part of your final answer.

If you find a mistake when checking your work, put a neat line through it and write the correct version above or alongside.

Referring to the Text

PEE

It is very important, both in exams and in controlled assessment that you refer closely to the text. Every **point** you make about your text should be supported by **evidence**, which is then followed by an **explanation** of the evidence. You can easily remember this as **PEE**:

- **P**oint
- **E**vidence
- **E**xplanation

Evidence

For your evidence you must refer to the text, whether you have it in front of you or not. Your evidence can be in the form of a paraphrase or a direct quotation.

Paraphrasing means putting something into your own words. It is useful if you cannot remember the exact words from the text and cannot look them up, either because you do not have the text with you or because it would take too long to find a quotation.

If you are writing about a longer text, such as a novel, there are times when you might not need a quotation because you are writing about an incident and the exact wording is not important. For example:

> Lydia clearly does not think much about her family's reputation. When she returns from London with Wickham she does not express any shame at her behaviour, but boasts about being married. This might be shocking to the reader, who knows the distress she has caused and how scandalous her behaviour would be considered.

Using Quotations

There are three ways to set out your quotations. Which method you use depends on the length of the quotation and how it fits into your sentence.

1 If your quotation consists of just a few words (or even one word) and fits naturally into the sentence without spoiling the sense, you simply put it in inverted commas (also known as 'quotation marks'):

> At the start of the soliloquy, Juliet refers to 'love-performing night', but it later becomes 'a sober suited matron all in black'. This reflects the change in her mood as she waits for Romeo.
> (*Romeo and Juliet* Act 3 scene 2)

2 If the quotation will not fit into your sentence but is fairly short (no more than one line of verse or 40 words of prose), put a colon (:) before the quotation, continue on the same line and use inverted commas:

> Benvolio passionately asserts that he is telling the truth: 'this is the truth, or let Benvolio die'. The strength of his language shows his anxiety about what the Prince might do.
> (*Romeo and Juliet* Act 3 scene 1)

3 If you want to use a longer quotation, leave a line and indent. You must indent the whole quotation and, when quoting verse, end the lines where they end in the original. You do not need to use inverted commas:

> This opposition will inevitably cause problems for the lovers and Juliet expresses her dilemma:
>
> > My only love sprung from my only hate!
> > Too early seen unknown, and known too late!
> > (*Romeo and Juliet* Act 1 scene 5)
>
> The use of paradox emphasises her confusion.

Helpful Hints

Only put words taken from the text inside the inverted commas.

Make sure you spell and punctuate exactly as in the text.

During an exam, method 1 is usually the best to use. You are more likely to remember significant words and short phrases.

Unit 1: Exploring Modern Texts

Unit 1: Section A

Everybody will take Unit 1: Exploring Modern Texts. However, not everyone will study the same texts.

The next section of this book focuses on Section A. Many of the topics covered in this section will also apply to Section B, but there are some important differences between the two sections. Pages 32–39 concentrate on Section B.

All the examples given in this book will be taken from texts on the examination board's 'set book' list.

Section A: Modern Prose or Drama

At the beginning of your course you (or, more probably, your teacher) will have decided which text to study. The choice is quite wide so there is plenty of scope for choosing a text that you will enjoy and which reflects the interests of your class.

If you choose to study the short stories in the AQA Anthology *Sunlight on the Grass* you should study all seven.

Alternatively, you could study one of these prose texts:
- *Lord of the Flies* by William Golding.
- *Martyn Pig* by Kevin Brooks.
- *The Woman in Black* by Susan Hill.
- *Touching the Void* by Joe Simpson.

If you prefer drama you have a choice of five plays:
- *Under Milk Wood* by Dylan Thomas.
- *The Crucible* by Arthur Miller.
- *Kindertransport* by Diane Samuels.
- *An Inspector Calls* by J.B. Priestley.
- *Deoxyribonucleic Acid (DNA)* by Dennis Kelly.

When you write about your chosen text you will be expected to look at the following:
- **Ideas, themes and issues:** This means what the text is about, i.e. not the story but what the text makes us think about.
- **Characters**: The people in the text, what they are like, how they act and react, and why.
- **Settings:** Where and when the action happens.
- **Language and techniques:** How the writer gets all these things across to the reader using language, form and structure.

One of the first things you might want to think about is **genre.** You will find this word used a lot in English classes. It is a French word and simply means 'type' or 'kind'.

What kind of text are you reading and how does this affect the way it is written and the way you respond to it?

There are many different genres of fiction. *Martyn Pig*, for example, was written for teenagers, but draws on the detective genre, while *The Woman in Black* might be described as a 'ghost story.' And what about the non-fiction texts, e.g. *Touching the Void*? The story is as exciting as anything in fiction, but does knowing that it really happened make a difference to how you react to it?

Drama texts require a slightly different approach because they were not written to be read, but to be performed.

Modern Texts: Ideas, Themes and Issues

What are Ideas, Themes and Issues?

Ideas, themes and issues are what the text is about. This does not mean writing about what happens – if you simply re-tell the story, you will not be able to gain a grade C or above, no matter how well you tell it!

You need to think about what matters to the writer, as shown through the story and characters. What is the writer trying to say to you, the reader or the audience? What does the text make you think about?

To get you started thinking about this, try summarising, in one sentence, what you think the text is about. For example:
- *Lord of the Flies* is about what happens when a group of young boys are stranded on an island without any adults.
- *The Crucible* is about the Salem witch trials.
- *Martyn Pig* is about a boy who kills his father.

If you have studied a different text or the short stories, write a similar sentence about the text(s) you have studied.

Now, ask yourself why the writer might want you to read about this situation and what it makes you think about. By moving away from the situation and on to the themes, try to come up with an alternative answer to the question 'What is it about?'. You could use a spider diagram or a list.

For example:
- *Lord of the Flies* is about…
  - growing up
  - civilisation
  - bullying
  - leadership
  - what boys are really like
  - what humans are really like.

- *The Crucible* is about…
  - telling the truth
  - marriage
  - the importance of reputation
  - history
  - paranoia
  - authority
  - teenage girls.

telling the truth		love and trust
father and son relationships	**Martyn Pig is about…**	death
detective stories		right and wrong

Some of the same themes crop up again and again in modern prose and drama. The set texts have been chosen partly because the examiners think people of your age will identify with them and will be interested in the ideas and issues brought up.

In literature there are more questions than answers. The following questions might get you thinking about the ideas and issues in your text:
- Is it ever right to kill someone?
- What would happen if there were no adults?
- Can you trust anyone?
- Are children innocent?
- Do children need both their parents?
- What do we mean by right and wrong?
- How far are we influenced by our backgrounds?
- Can we change our own lives for the better?
- How far are we responsible for other people?
- Do ghosts exist?
- Should you always tell the truth?
- Is it sometimes better to forget the past?
- When should we put other people's interests before our own?
- What should we do to survive?
- Is there a God?

Try jotting down as many questions as you can that your text might make someone ask. Then try to find more than one answer to each question, backing up your answers with evidence from the text.

Modern Texts: Ideas, Themes and Issues

Presenting Ideas, Themes and Issues

Once you have identified the main themes, ideas and issues in a text, you need to consider how they are presented and what the writer might be saying about them.

Writers very rarely tell us directly what they think. Sometimes their attitudes and opinions might be implied by what their characters say and do. More often they want to make us think by presenting us with questions to which there may be more than one answer.

Sometimes a writer uses the story's **narrator** to reflect on what is happening and what this might mean. For example, Martyn Pig shares with the reader his thoughts about what he has done. He talks about very big issues, such as whether God exists and whether killing someone is always wrong. Carla, in *My Polish Teacher's Tie*, also wonders about whether she is doing the right thing when she doesn't tell Steve that she is not a teacher. As readers, we may agree with what the narrator is saying or we may take the opposite point of view.

Ideas and issues are also presented through dialogue between different characters. Martyn discusses ideas with Alex, and in *The Darkness Out There*, Sandra discusses with Kerry what they have discovered about Mrs Rutter. Different characters may have very different points of view about what is going on. In this way, we are given more than one viewpoint on an issue. We can weigh up these different viewpoints, perhaps deciding that we agree with one of them or perhaps being able to see that both characters have a point.

In every story the main character(s) go on a journey. At the end of the story they are different from how they were at the beginning. They change because of what happens to them and what their experiences teach them about themselves and the world they live in. Like the characters, readers respond to actions and events with a wide range of emotions. On reflection, we might wonder why we have reacted like this, making us think about our own assumptions and beliefs, just as the characters think about theirs.

Remember, there is no one right answer when you are discussing the ideas, themes and issues in a text. This is because every reader reacts differently to what he or she is reading. We all have our own opinions, but if you can understand other possible points of view and take them into account in your answers, you are more likely to get a good mark. You might consider several points of view and decide which one you agree with – or you might decide that they are equally valid. Either way, don't be afraid to say what you think the text is about.

Modern Texts: Ideas, Themes and Issues

Presenting Ideas, Themes and Issues in Drama

Much of what we have said about the presentation of ideas, themes and issues in prose texts also applies to plays. However, there are certain differences.

The stage is a **visual medium**. It is all about showing, not telling. We discover the themes of the play through what happens in front of our eyes. The image of the girl and her mother sitting among the bags and boxes at the beginning of *Kindertransport* shows the reality of their situation far more effectively than any number of words could.

... in *The Crucible*, Elizabeth Proctor tells a lie for the ... her life in the mistaken belief that she is helping

her husband, the audience is as stunned as he is. One of the major themes of the play is captured in a moment.

Under Milk Wood, written for radio, has a narrator. The narrator speaks what would, in a conventional stage play, be the stage directions, as well as describing scenes as the narrator of a story might. He does not, however, express ideas and opinions.

In a play, the writer does not usually have a **voice** through which to express his or her own ideas and opinions, although sometimes – as in *The Crucible* – there is some discussion of the issues in the **stage directions** of a published text. You may also have access to interviews or articles where the writers have expressed their personal views. Nevertheless, when you watch a play, you see and hear only what the characters do and say.

Sometimes a character will speak his or her thoughts directly to the audience, in a **soliloquy** or **aside**. Traditionally, a soliloquy tells us what the character is actually thinking. We know that he or she is telling the truth. A character might discuss ideas and issues in a speech to the audience, just as the first person narrator of a story might allow us to share his or her thoughts.

More often, ideas, themes and issues are presented through dialogue, just as they can be presented through conversations in novels and short stories. By listening to these conversations we are made aware of each character's background and personality, and of the characters' attitudes towards each other. This influences us when we are considering the ideas that are being discussed on stage.

We can hear as many different points of view on an issue as there are actors on stage. Almost everyone in *The Crucible* has a view on witchcraft and the trials – these are very argumentative people! In *An Inspector Calls*, members of the family react very differently to the news of Eva Smith's death. We can weigh up these different viewpoints, perhaps deciding that we agree with one of them or perhaps being able to see that several characters have a point.

Like the characters, the audience responds to what happens with a wide range of emotions. One audience will include people who respond very differently from each other to the ideas presented on stage. Their reactions might make them think about their own assumptions and beliefs, just as the characters think about theirs.

Modern Texts: Characters

What Do We Mean by 'Character'?

Books are about people. The word **character** can simply refer to a person (real or invented) in a book or play. But when we discuss people's characters, we are talking about who they are and what they are like.

Protagonist or Hero?

Most texts feature one main character, often called the **protagonist**. This is the person that the story is about. It is his/her journey that we share when we read the text – and when the story finishes we can see how much that person has changed because of what has happened to him/her.

Who would you say is the protagonist of the text you have studied? In *Martyn Pig* it is obviously Martyn – the novel is even named after him. But the protagonist, and narrator, of the book *The Woman in Black* is Arthur Kipps, not the mysterious woman who gives the novel its name. John Proctor is clearly the protagonist of *The Crucible*, even though there are several other very strong characters in the play. But who, if anyone, is the protagonist of *An Inspector Calls*? And what about *Under Milk Wood*?

Sometimes you might hear the main character referred to as a **hero**. What do you think of when you hear the word 'hero'?

- Somebody extraordinary, with special powers?
- Somebody with special qualities, such as courage?
- Someone with high moral values?
- An ordinary person who does something extraordinary when called upon?

Does John Proctor in *The Crucible* reach heroic status when he stands up to his accusers? In *Touching the Void*, does the way Joe Simpson managed to survive after his accident make him a hero? Or was he just doing what anyone would do, trying to stay alive? Can Ralph in *Lord of the Flies* be described as a hero? He certainly shows qualities which many readers would admire, yet he has weaknesses which might help earn our sympathy.

The main character in your text might be none of these. He/she might just be an ordinary person with whom the reader can identify or sympathise. Martyn Pig seems to be just an ordinary teenager, but he gets caught up in a chain of extraordinary events that he has to deal with. He does not do anything especially admirable – in fact, many readers might think he has brought his problems on himself by making a series of poor decisions, e.g. not calling the police immediately – but we can imagine ourselves in his position and wonder what we would do.

Sandra in *The Darkness Out There* and the boy in *Compass and Torch* are also quite ordinary, unexceptional people. Perhaps they even represent the 'typical' teenager or eight-year-old (the boy is not even given a name – he could be anyone). Their experiences are not very dramatic and might not bring out extraordinary qualities in them – but they learn from them and grow up a little because of them.

An experience that changes a character is sometimes called an **epiphany**. Short stories often centre on a character's epiphany, whereas a novel tends to show the character developing over a longer period through a series of experiences.

Modern Texts: Characters

Antagonist or Villain?

In some texts the protagonist might have an enemy or just someone who gets in his / her way. A character like this can be called an **antagonist** and can be developed in as much detail as the protagonist. Antagonists are not necessarily bad or unpleasant – although they can be – but they cause problems for the protagonists and stand in their way – stopping them, or trying to stop them, achieving what they want.

Think about the characters in the text you have studied. Is there anyone you might call an antagonist? If so, why?

Try comparing two strong characters in a text, for example Joe and Simon in *Touching the Void*. Make a list of their differences and similarities.

Other Characters

Some texts (especially the short stories) have very few characters, while others contain a huge range of people.

When you look at these characters, you should think about what they are like, just as you might think about a real person. You might look at the following:

- Age
- Gender
- Social class
- Physical appearance
- Personality traits
- Attitudes and opinions.

Then look a little deeper and think about why the writer has included a particular character. It takes quite a lot of effort to create a character. Every character, however minor, is there for a purpose. You should think about what that purpose might be. Usually it is about how they relate to the protagonist and / or how they move the story on. What is Piggy's role in *Lord of the Flies*? Why has Dean been included in *Martyn Pig*? What is the point of Mrs Kenward in *My Polish Teacher's Tie?*

How Characters are Presented in Prose Texts

There are four main ways in which writers tell us about their characters:

- What the writer or narrator says about a character.
- What a character says.
- What other people say about a character.
- How a character acts and reacts.

What the Writer / Narrator Says

In a third person narrative the writer will often describe the characters' physical appearance, something about their background and their personalities. We can usually rely on this information. For example, we can take anything that William Golding says about the boys' lives before the crash to be true. However, you should beware of first person narratives! Martyn might describe Alex's appearance and mannerisms accurately in *Martyn Pig*, but does he really understand her?

What a Character Says

First person narrators often have a lot to say about themselves. They might give us useful clues about themselves, but are we always good judges of our own character? Characters can also reveal a lot about themselves unknowingly by the way they speak and what they say.

What Other People say About a Character

Characters often comment on each other and can give us differing views. We might make a judgement about who is right or we might think the differing views are all valid.

How a Character Acts and Reacts

We probably learn most about fictional characters, just as we do about real people, by their actions. Just as important as how they act is how they react to what others do and say.

How Characters are Presented in Drama

One of the most important things to remember when reading a play is that it was not written to be read. It was written to be performed.

For actors and directors the text is a 'script' and it is not really finished until it is performed in the theatre. What you see on stage is not just the writer's idea of the character, but the actors' and the director's.

Different actors can interpret the same character in different ways. If possible, you should go to see a live production of your chosen play. When plays become set texts they are often revived in the theatre.

You might also be able to watch a filmed version or listen to a CD. There is a very good, easily available, recent film version of *The Crucible* and a good (if rather old) version of *An Inspector Calls*. The classic BBC radio

Modern Texts: Characters

version and film versions of *Under Milk Wood* are easy to get hold of. If you can see more than one version of a play, you will be able to compare different performances and this will help you to write about how it is possible to interpret a character in different ways.

Actors use the text to gain an understanding of their characters, but they can make many choices about how they present that character.

Actors sometimes feel that they need to 'know' more about a character than what is actually presented to them in the script. So they 'read between the lines', looking for clues about why the character might act in a certain way and what sort of life he / she might have had before the play begins.

For example, one actor playing Abigail Williams in *The Crucible* might think the clue to her character lies in what she says happened to her parents, while another actor might think Abigail makes that up to frighten the other girls.

Two actors playing Mr Birling in *An Inspector Calls* might differ about the effect his humble background has on the way he acts towards his family.

When you have watched a performance of your play, make a note of how the actors playing various roles use the tools at their disposal to present characters.

Think about whether, if you were directing, you would advise the actors to do things differently. Amongst an actor's tools are the following:

- **Voice:** accent, tone of voice, emphasis, pitch and volume all tell us something about what a character is thinking or feeling.
- **Facial expression:** even when they are not speaking, actors convey a lot of emotion through their expressions.
- **Movement:** the way people move can tell us a lot, not only about their personalities, but also about their moods and how they relate to others.
- **Posture:** how he / she stands or sits 'gives away' a lot about a person.

If you get a chance in class, or when revising with friends, you could try performing a scene from a play. You could play the characters in as many different ways as possible, even quite silly ones.

Discuss which interpretation is most appropriate and why.

Modern Texts: Characters

Keeping a Character Log

Whether you are studying a play or a prose text, it is a good idea to keep a **character log** as you read your text. This is especially useful when you read your text for revision. You could copy the example below, or you could make up your own design. Print off a few sheets for all the characters you think are important. As you read, jot down brief notes under the appropriate headings.

Here is an example of a partly completed character log:

Name: Evelyn (*Kindertransport*)	
Reference	**What it Tells Us**
What the writer says about her: *'English middle-class woman. In her fifties.'* (list of characters p.2)	She has become totally English. No-one would know her background.
What she says: *'Nothing is too good for my daughter'* (p.6)	She is proud of her daughter and wants her to look good.
'There is nothing to talk about' (p.42)	She does not want to talk about the past.
What others say about her: *'Your things are beautiful'* (Faith p.6)	Her daughter admires her taste. Perhaps material things are important to her.
'I've found some of my own things. I'd no idea she's kept them' (Faith p.14)	Faith does not expect her to be sentimental.
How she acts: *'She polishes glasses to give to her daughter'* (p.8–9)	She likes things clean, neat and orderly.
How she reacts: *'She avoids discussing her past by leaving the room'* (p.42)	She continues to avoid her past.

When you look back at your character logs, you will see that you have a collection of useful references to the text as well as notes about their significance. Even if you cannot remember the exact quotations, these references will be useful when you come to write your exam answer.

Modern Texts: Settings

Settings

Every text we read is its own little world – a world created by the writer and inhabited by the characters. Sometimes this world seems familiar, very like the world in which we live. Sometimes it is like the 'real' world that the writer knows or knows about, but which might seem strange to many readers. Sometimes it is a world of fantasy, invented by the writer.

So how do writers decide where and when to set their stories and plays? And what difference does the setting make to our enjoyment and understanding of their texts?

Time

The time when a text is set is very important. This could mean the time of day or time of year, but also whether it is set in the present, the past or even the future.

Martyn Pig is set around Christmas, while most of *The Woman in Black* takes place in November. What difference does this make to the atmosphere and tone of the stories? Even the time of day when a particular event happens can make´a difference. For example, in *Compass and Torch* the mood changes as the night draws in.

Many of the texts you might study for Unit 1 are set at the time when they were written, for example, *Compass and Torch, My Polish Teacher's Tie, The Darkness Out There* and *Martyn Pig*. Although none of them are very precise about when they are set, we can tell from the descriptions of everyday life that they are not far distant from our own time.

A present day setting might make us feel that we are in a familiar world where people are just like us and act like us. But the familiarity of the setting can make it all the more disturbing when something out of the ordinary occurs. For example, a girl setting out to help an old lady would not expect to hear about a horrible death many years earlier (as in *The Darkness Out There)* and we would not expect an ordinary teenager to become involved in murder (as in *Martyn Pig*).

In *Lord of the Flies*, William Golding takes this idea to the extreme by taking middle-class English boys of his time (the 1950s) and imagining how they would behave in extreme circumstances.

It is important to be aware of the attitudes and ideas that were current when the novel was written.

The Second World War caused many people to question the ideas that they had grown up with. In view of some of the horrific events of the war, they wondered whether mankind really was civilised. Are any of us really any better than those who killed millions during the war? In extreme circumstances who would we act like – Ralph or Jack?

Modern Texts: Settings

The Past

Some writers choose an historical setting. From these texts we can learn about how people lived in the past, their beliefs, assumptions and values. But, remember that they were written recently and so the events are seen from a modern point of view.

Both *The Crucible* and *An Inspector Calls* are set long before they were written. J.B. Priestley wrote *An Inspector Calls* after the Second World War, but set it before the First World War. Therefore, even his first audience had the benefit of hindsight when watching the play. Mr Birling talks confidently in Act 1 about the future of Britain, but in fact things turned out very differently from his predictions. The writer and the audience know this, so Priestley can be said to be using **dramatic irony**. Inspector Goole warns about the possible consequences for the world if people refuse to take responsibility for each other. He could be referring to the coming of the First World War, but also to the Second World War. We know that Priestley, like many others of his time, was a great supporter of social change. That is why Inspector Goole is often seen as a sort of 'ghost from the future'.

Unlike *An Inspector Calls*, *The Crucible* is based on real events. Arthur Miller's research was very thorough and, although he changed one or two details, the play is an accurate account of what happened in Salem. It is worth finding out about the real events and considering how and why Miller may have changed some details.

However, when the play was first produced in the 1950s it was seen by many as being as much about current events as historical ones. Miller himself had been called before a government committee which was looking for communists – these hearings became known as 'witch hunts'.

Audiences today might not be aware of what was going on at the time when the play was first performed, but it may remind them of more recent events that they have heard about. If the play had been set in the 1950s it may not have been as popular or have been as relevant to later generations.

It is quite common in short stories and novels for the writer to go back in time by using a character's memories. Arthur Kipps, the narrator of *The Woman in Black*, starts his story in what is for him the present day. He is middle-aged, comfortable and surrounded by his family. When the children start to tell ghost stories he feels the need to write his account of something that happened many years before.

Similarly, the most dramatic events of *The Darkness Out There* took place a long time before the story begins. This time the story is told to Sandra and Kerry (and to the reader) by Mrs Rutter.

'Flashbacks' are less common in drama, but are used in an original way by Diane Samuels in *Kindertransport*. Here, the story of Eva and her mother is told by having that story and the story of the grown-up Eva (now Evelyn) unfold in parallel, in alternate scenes. This helps to give the audience a sense of how our past is impossible to escape.

Place

Where a story or novel is set is just as important as when it is set. The setting can help to put the text in context by telling you about the society that the characters live in. Look at the places where your text is set and ask these questions:

- Is it urban or rural?
- Is it a thriving community or a depressed one?
- Is it a place where the same families have lived for generations, or a place where people tend not to stay for long?
- Are the characters happy or unhappy to be living there? Why?

Now look at the more detailed descriptions of the places where the action takes place.

Looking around people's houses can tell you a lot about them. There are detailed descriptions of Martyn's home in *Martyn Pig*, which tell us a lot about Martyn, his father and their life together. The description of Arthur's house at the beginning of *The Woman in Black* tells us about his comfortable, middle-class family life.

However, people's surroundings can be misleading. Mrs Rutter's cottage in *The Darkness Out There* seems comfortable and welcoming, in contrast to her account of what happened in the woods during the war.

Often writers describe natural landscapes. The real places described in *Touching the Void*, thousands of miles from home, are awe-inspiring and potentially fatal. The island in *Lord of the Flies* seems at first to be like a tropical paradise, but later it is threatening and eerie.

Sometimes descriptions of landscapes and the weather are used to reflect the feelings and emotions of the characters. For example:

- A stormy night might reflect their inner conflicts and strong emotions.
- The sun suddenly appearing could represent hope.

This technique is sometimes called **pathetic fallacy.** Other techniques you might look for are the following:

- The use of **adjectives.**
- The use of **metaphors** and **similes.**
- The **personification** of aspects of nature.
- The use of telling **details.**

Preparation Task

Skim through your chosen text and see if you can find a passage where the writer describes a place in detail. What techniques is he/she using to convey the atmosphere and significance of that place?

Stage Sets

When considering the setting of a play, you should think about what the stage set would be like.

Some plays, like *An Inspector Calls,* include very detailed descriptions of the set. Priestley's description of the Birlings' house tells us a lot about their lives. You should feel free to quote from such stage directions in your exam. However, you should also bear in mind that the designer of a new production can ignore the directions in the text or adapt them.

The stage directions for *Kindertransport* simply refer to a 'dusty storage room'. Both the 'present day' scenes and the 'flashback' scenes take place here, with no set changes. This underlines the relationship of the present to the past.

Preparation Task

If you are studying a play, why not try designing your own stage set? What does your set say about the themes of the play, its characters and their lives?

Modern Texts: Language and Techniques

Language

Writers use language in many different ways to achieve effects. Their themes, settings and characters dictate the language they use.

Standard and Non-Standard English

You are probably used to these terms from your study of English Language. **Standard English** is the language we use when writing official documents, essays or formal letters. It uses correct grammar and standard vocabulary, avoiding slang, dialect and abbreviation. It has a formal tone.

Non-standard English gives writing an informal tone. It can be chatty, friendly and sound more like speech. Regional dialect words, slang, abbreviations and 'incorrect' grammar are acceptable. We might use informal or non-standard English in letters to friends, notes, emails or diary entries.

Think about the 'tone' of your text and whether it is formal or informal.

First person narratives (see page 26) are more likely to be informal and use non-standard English. *Martyn Pig* is written in a very chatty tone, as if Martyn is actually talking to the reader. He even says things like, 'I know what you're thinking', which draws the reader into his world.

On the other hand, Arthur Kipps in *The Woman in Black,* uses a more formal tome. We would expect this not only because of his age and status, but also because he tells us in the first chapter that he is writing the tale to be read after his death.

Archaic and Specialised Diction

Archaic words and phrases are those that have fallen out of use. English has changed a great deal over the last thousand years.

Therefore, the older your text the more likely you are to find archaic diction. You would not expect to find archaic language in a recently written text. However, some modern texts are set in the past.

You might find archaic words and phrases in *The Crucible* (set in the 1690s) or even in *An Inspector Calls* and *The Woman in Black* (both set in the early twentieth century).

Modern Texts: Language and Techniques

Specialised or **technical** vocabulary means the kind of words and phrases that you might find used by people with an advanced knowledge of certain subjects (e.g. medicine, law or mechanics) and which ordinary people would not normally understand. Joe Simpson uses a lot of specialised terminology connected with mountaineering in *Touching the Void*, yet he does not provide a glossary to explain these words. Why do you think this is?

Negative and Positive Diction

At certain points in a text you might find a lot of words and phrases that have either negative or positive **connotations** (associations). This type of diction will change the mood and atmosphere of the piece. Think about why certain words or phrases have this effect on the reader.

Sounds

Sometimes the sound of the words used is important. Terms like **alliteration**, **assonance** and **onomatopoeia** are often used when discussing poetry, but prose writers should also be very aware of the sound of the words they use. You should look especially for the effect of sounds in descriptive passages.

Imagery

Visual imagery is very important in prose texts; writers 'paint pictures' in words. This not only allows the reader to know what a place looks likes but it also conveys an atmosphere or a sense of how a character is feeling. Look at how the writer uses **metaphors** and **similes,** and how they affect your response.

Syntax and Punctuation

Syntax refers to the order in which words are used. The term includes sentence structure and grammatical forms.

The length of sentences can be worth commenting on. Very short or even incomplete sentences can be used for dramatic effect. Long sentences are often used to express complex ideas or give detailed descriptions.

Most stories are told in the active voice, because they are about people doing things. If the writer uses the passive voice it makes the text less personal, more formal and perhaps a little more objective.

Punctuation can make a difference. Are there a lot of question marks (perhaps to make the reader ask questions) or exclamation marks (to convey excitement or strong emotions)? Does the writer use dashes or use punctuation in an unusual or original way?

Dialogue

Apart from the stage directions, plays consist entirely of dialogue, but many novels and short stories also contain a lot of dialogue. The ways in which the characters speak tell us a lot about them. For example:

- **Age:** the young people in *An Inspector Calls* use 'modern' slang.
- **Status:** in *The Crucible,* Mary Warren is the Proctors' servant and so addresses them respectfully.
- **Personality:** Mr Birling in *An Inspector Calls* is confident and bombastic. His language reflects this.
- **Regional background:** the characters in *Under Milk Wood* use words and phrases that are typical of South Wales.
- **Ethnic background:** In *Kindertransport,* young Eva and her mother speak in German.

People also change the way they speak according to the situation they are in and who they are talking to. For example, Act Three of *The Crucible* takes place in court. Therefore, much of the language is formal and legal.

In most plays the dialogue is naturalistic, imitating real-life speech. However, sometimes writers deliberately use speech that is different in some way from real speech. *Under Milk Wood* is an obvious example of this, as the characters speak in verse. Other plays may have dialogue that is non-naturalistic in a different way.

You should consider all these aspects of language when you are looking at prose texts written in the first person.

Helpful Hint

A lot of the things you might say about language apply equally to fiction, non-fiction and drama texts. However, if you are writing about a play, always remember that it is written to be performed and refer to the effect on the **audience**, not the reader.

Modern Texts: Language and Techniques

Narrative Style

A **narrative** is a story and a **narrator** is a person who tells a story. Plays do not normally have a narrator, but in a novel, short story or non-fiction text there is always a narrator. Sometimes we are conscious of the narrator's voice and sometimes we hardly notice it. But it is always there and can make a huge difference to how we read the text.

Most texts are written in the **first person** (I) or the **third person** (he / she / they). Make sure you are clear about whether your text is written in the first or third person.

First Person Narrative

Who is telling the story? A first person narrator is usually also the main character in the story. This means that the story we read is written entirely or mainly from that character's point of view.

However, writers occasionally include sections that give another character's point of view. For example, *Touching the Void* contains sections written from the point of view of Simon Yates. This means we can read parts of the story that the main narrator did not witness, and can also get an alternative viewpoint. This overcomes a potential problem with first person narrative – that one person cannot know and understand everything that is going on.

In fiction, however, writers frequently use first person narrators *because* they do not want us to know everything. Martyn Pig shares everything he knows with the reader, but it gradually becomes clear that he does not know the whole story and we learn, as he does, that all is not as it seems. Martyn is a **naïve** narrator. The writer uses his naivety to 'trick' us, so that we – like Martyn – are surprised by the way things turn out.

In *My Polish Teacher's Tie* and *The Woman in Black*, we are also kept guessing about how things will turn out. We **empathise** with the narrators, knowing all their thoughts and sharing their hopes and fears. We live through the experiences with them.

Third Person Narrative

The advantage of a third person narrative is that the writer is not limited to one person's thoughts and feelings. Sometimes these narratives are written as if someone (the writer) is watching the action from a neutral point of view. At other times, they will share with us the thoughts and feelings of the characters.

Often the writer tells the story through the main character, so that we tend to see things from his / her point of view. Most of *Lord of the Flies* is seen from Ralph's point of view, while in *Compass and Torch* the story is seen mainly through the boy's eyes. However, in a third person narrative, the writer has the power to read the minds of all his / her characters. So we do share some of the thoughts and feelings of Piggy or Simon in *Lord of the Flies* or the father in *Compass and Torch*.

Because the narrator knows everything that goes on and can choose to share with the readers anything he / she wants to, these narrators are sometimes said to be **omniscient** (all knowing).

Modern Texts: Language and Techniques

Structure

Story Structure

A story must have a beginning, middle and end, but for a story to work it needs a little more. Most stories, in whatever form they are told, have a similar structure.

1 The story starts by telling us something about the characters and the world they live in. This is sometimes called **exposition.**

2 Then, something happens to change things, such as Martyn's father dying in *Martyn Pig* or Carla hearing about the Polish teacher in *My Polish Teacher's Tie*. This is sometimes called the **inciting incident.**

3 As the story progresses things happen that change the direction of the story. Examples of this are Sandra meeting Kerry in *The Darkness Out There* and Simon cutting the rope in *Touching the Void.* There could be several of these events.

4 Towards the end the story reaches a **climax.** This can be a happy ending or a sad ending, or one where we are not sure which it is.

5 The climax does not usually come at the very end of the book or play. It is often followed by a short section where we can reflect on what has happened and compare the way things are now to how they were at the start.

Think about whether your text fits this pattern and decide which are the key moments in the plot, i.e. the events that change things.

Preparation Task

A good way to revise story structure or plot is to write a 'mini saga'. Re-tell the story, using only 50 words, but making sure that you include all the most important parts of the story.

Text Organisation

Writers organise their stories in different ways. The most straightforward way of telling a story is **chronologically** (in the order in which it happened). But writers can use other techniques, for example:

- In *The Woman in Black*, Arthur explains to the reader why he is telling the story before going back to the time when it started.
- *Martyn Pig* tells his story in chronological order, dividing the story into days. He then adds an **epilogue,** which is 'written' a year later.
- *Compass and Torch* is mostly in the present tense, but there are short sections in past tense as the boy recalls the events before he sets off on the camping trip.
- *Kindertransport* tells two stories chronologically, in alternating scenes.
- *An Inspector Calls* has a twist at the end, when the story seems to start again with another telephone call.

You should also look at how the text is physically set out and divided up. Longer novels and non-fiction texts are usually divided into chapters. You should think about why the writers begin and end the chapters when they do. Sometimes, as in *Lord of the Flies* and *The Woman in Black*, the chapters have titles. Do not ignore these but think about what they mean.

Short stories, too, sometimes have internal divisions. An example of this is *Compass and Torch*.

Plays are traditionally divided into acts and scenes. The end of an act would normally indicate where there would be an interval in the theatre. At the time *An Inspector Calls* was written it was common to have two intervals. Now it is rare, so most plays are written in two acts. Playwrights tend to end each act on a turning point in the plot.

Under Milk Wood was originally a radio play. Therefore it consists of lots of very short scenes linked by narration and marked by sound effects.

Preparation Task

You could revise text organisation by making a 'storyboard'. Use between eight and twelve 'frames' and in each one write a short sentence and do an illustration.

Modern Texts Section A: Exam Tips

This exam is called **Unit 1: Exploring Modern Texts**. It is in two sections.

For Section A you are allowed to use unannotated texts. That means copies of your chosen texts that have no notes at all, whether on the text itself or on loose sheets.

- You may be given a 'clean' copy of the text in the exam room.
- You may be told to bring your own text. In this case, it is up to you to erase all notes from the book, whether made by you or by somebody else.

Before the exam make sure that you:

- Know your text well – you may only have read it once in class, but you should have read it another two or three times on your own.
- Read the notes you have taken or been given in class and make sure you understand them.
- Come up with your own ideas about the texts – the examiner wants to know what you think, not what your teacher thinks.
- Identify and put right errors that you know you make in punctuation, grammar and spelling.
- Complete the exam preparation and exam practice tasks given in this section of the guide.
- Perfect the PEE technique.
- Are able to write confidently about...
  - ideas, themes and issues
  - characters
  - settings
  - language and technique.

In the exam, make sure that you do the following:

- Be aware of the time: you should spend **45 minutes** on Section A. It is helpful to spend about 5 minutes planning what you are going to write.
- Quickly find the questions on the text you have studied. Do not even think about reading the questions on texts you have not studied in class.
- Read the two questions on your text carefully. Choose one that you fully understand and you feel you can answer well.
- If there are bullet points (more likely in Foundation Tier questions) keep them in mind and make sure you cover all the points made in them.

If you are writing about the **short stories:**

- Remember that your question is in two parts – effectively two short essays. Answer both parts.
- Divide your time equally between the two parts (20 minutes for each).
- For part (b) choose the story you are going to write about carefully. Make sure that it is the right story for the question and that you can write confidently on it.
- Remember that you only need to write about one story for each part of the question. You do not need to compare stories.

Helpful Hint

Make sure you use the correct terminology when you mention your text. Is it a story, a novel or a play?

Modern Texts: Exam Practice

Exam questions often contain key words or commands, which tell you what to do. If you understand these you will be able to stay focused on the task and give better answers:

- The word '**how**' tells you that you need to focus on the writer's techniques, not just the content of the text. The question might ask you how the writer **presents** or **conveys** a theme or a character.
- You might be asked to write about the **ways** in which something or someone is **used** in a text.
- You could also be asked about the **significance** of something or someone. If you are asked about the significance of a character, you do not just write about what the character does, but about how the character is used to convey ideas.
- Sometimes a question will start with a quotation about the text and then ask you how you **respond** to it or whether, and how far, you **agree** with it.

Practice Questions

Answer one of the following questions in 45 minutes. If none of them is about your text, try adapting the question. When you have finished, ask a teacher or a fellow student to grade your answer.

Question 1

Part a)

Write about the ways in which Lively uses the idea of the woods to present ideas in *The Darkness Out There*.

Write about:
- What people feel about the woods and what has happened there.
- The methods Lively uses to show their significance.

Part b)

Go on to write about how nature is used in one other story from the anthology.

Write about:
- The aspects of nature described in the story and what they mean.
- The methods the writer uses to show their meaning.

Question 2

'*Lord of the Flies* proves that there is no such thing as a civilised society'. How do you respond to this view of Golding's novel?

Question 3

How effective do you find the ending of *The Woman in Black*?

Question 4

How does Samuels present relationships between mothers and daughters in *Kindertransport*?

Write about:
- The different mother / daughter relationships presented in the play.
- The methods Samuels uses to present these relationships.

Question 5

What is the significance of Eva Smith in *An Inspector Calls*?

Preparation Task

Try to come up with as many likely questions as you can for your own text. Then answer each of them in a single sentence before choosing one to answer in full.

On the following two pages you will find a...
- writing frame for one of the questions above, which will give you an idea of how to structure an answer
- partial answer to another question, with some key points highlighted.

Developing Your Answer

Question 4

How does Samuels present relationships between mothers and daughters in *Kindertransport*?

Write about:

- The different mother / daughter relationships presented in the play.
- The methods Samuels uses to present these relationships.

When answering a question like this, you need to make sure you cover all the mother / daughter relationships in the play and that you comment on how each of them is presented.

The easiest way of doing this is to take each relationship in turn, explaining what you think the relationship is like and how it is shown through the way the women speak and act towards each other.

Introduction: State what you are going to do and refer back to the question.
→ The mother / daughter relationship is an important theme in 'Kindertransport'. Diane Samuels uses three generations of women to explore this theme...

Faith and Evelyn
→ In the scenes set in the present day, Faith discovers about her mother Evelyn's past. At first theirs might seem a typical relationship between a middle-class mother and her grown-up daughter...

Evelyn and Lil
→ Faith has been brought up to believe that Lil is her grandmother and, although Lil has gone along with this, she does not seem entirely happy with Evelyn not telling the truth to her daughter...

Lil and Eva
→ The 'flashback' scenes show us how this relationship developed, as we see Lil meet Eva for the first time. In this scene Eva speaks in German...

Eva and Helga
→ Eva's life with Lil is contrasted with her old life with Helga, her real mother. The play opens with Helga and Eva preparing for Eva's departure for England...

Conclusion
→ All these relationships are different but all show the strength of the bond between a mother and her daughter and the suffering caused when that bond is broken. At the end of the play, Evelyn says, 'Stay my little girl forever', but this is impossible... .

Developing Your Answer

Question 1

Part a)

Write about the ways in which Lively uses the idea of the woods to present ideas in *The Darkness Out There*.

Write about:

- What people feel about the woods and what has happened there.
- The methods Lively uses to show their significance.

When answering a question on the short stories, remember that you have to answer, separately, on two different stories. You only have a short time for each answer, so you have to get all your points across very quickly. You cannot afford to 'ramble'!

Introductory paragraph addresses the question and says what you are going to talk about

Connectives used to link paragraphs and sentences

PEE used effectively. Short quotations with explanations

Appropriate terminology used

Characters explored

Settings are explored throughout. This is the main focus of the whole answer

Techniques / form and structure discussed

Ideas, themes and issues explored

Effective conclusion

The image of the woods – or spinney – dominates 'The Darkness Out There'. Although Sandra never actually goes into the woods, she has lived nearby all her life and knows lots of stories about them. By the end of this story, she knows about something that really happened there and, because of it, feels differently about life.

Although the story is written in the third person, most of it is seen from Sandra's point of view and we know her feelings about Packer's End. It has represented different things for her at different times in her life. As a very young girl she imagined 'witches, wolves and tigers' in the wood. What Sandra is doing now, going to visit Mrs Rutter's cottage, reminds the reader of the story of Red Riding Hood, when the girl goes to visit her grandmother in the woods. Fairy tales were traditionally told to warn children of the dangers of the world. Dark woods, witches and wolves are symbolic of these dangers.

Later, as a teenager, Sandra and her friends worry more about what they read in the papers about assaults and rapes. It would seem sensible for a girl on her own to avoid lonely places, but Lively suggests that the tales of rape could be just as much 'fairy tales' as those about witches: 'People couldn't remember what her name was, exactly…Two enormous blokes, sort of gypsy types'. The vagueness of the description, reported in colloquial language like a piece of gossip, undermines the story that has just been told.

Now she is older and can take her mind off what might be in the woods by thinking of her future and of romance: she is portrayed as a 'typical' teenager with no special problems or concerns and a hopeful outlook on life. She is still aware of what people say about the German plane that crashed in the woods but she is able to dismiss it as 'creepy' – something unpleasant that does not affect her and that she would rather not think about.

However, when she is in Mrs Rutter's house, she is forced to think about it. Mrs Rutter seems like a stereotypical 'little old lady', but so was the witch who lured Hansel and Gretel into her gingerbread house. When she tells her story to Kerry and Sandra, they start to see her in a different light. She thinks she is 'lucky – right up beside the wood. Lovely it is in the spring', but the woods that night in 1942 were very different, 'rain teeming down and a raw November night'. The weather, contrasted with the sunny day when she tells the story, reflects the mood and atmosphere of that night during the war. The darkness and the inaccessibility of the woods add to the danger, but they also make it easier for Mrs Rutter and her sister to make their decision not to get help. The horror of the crash can be ignored if it is hidden in the woods.

Because of the story, the woods take on a different meaning. The teenagers are shocked by what they have heard. They have been shown a very different world from the one they live in now. It is a dark world, where an ordinary woman could leave a young man to die because of the hatred and bitterness she felt. They have seen the dark side of humanity.

At the end of the story, Sandra has grown up a bit, but growing up does not seem as attractive as when she was dreaming of beaches and romance. Packer's End does hold dark secrets, but not childish or silly ones. The symbolism of the wood has changed for Sandra and she knows it is not something you can ignore: 'The darkness was out there and it was part of you and you would never be without it, ever'. So, Penelope Lively uses the woods to explore the 'dark side' of human nature and suggests that when you grow up it is necessary to confront the darkness.

Modern Texts: Exploring Cultures

Section B: Exploring Cultures

The following eight pages focus on Section B of Unit 1, which is the compulsory examination. The texts you have studied for this part of the exam are modern prose texts. Therefore, everything that you read about the Section A texts also applies to Section B texts.

You need to look at the following:
• Ideas, themes and issues (see pages 14–16)
• Characters (see pages 17–20)
• Settings (see pages 21–23)
• Language and techniques (see pages 24–27)

However, there are two major differences:
• The texts are written by and about people from a range of cultural backgrounds. You need to show that you understand the importance of that culture in the text you have studied.
• You will be answering a different style of question. You will be given an extract from your text and asked to discuss it in detail before writing about the whole text.

As with Section A, there is a choice of texts. You will have studied one of the following texts:
• *Of Mice and Men* by John Steinbeck
• *Mister Pip* by Lloyd Jones
• *Purple Hibiscus* by Chimamanda Ngozi Adichie
• *To Kill a Mockingbird* by Harper Lee.

What is Meant by 'Culture'?

Culture can mean 'the arts', e.g. music, literature, drama, painting and sculpture. But when we talk about 'culture' in English it is used in a wider context. Culture refers to somebody's background and sense of identity. It is part of the setting of a text and part of the characters. Culture can in itself be one of the main themes and have a bearing on other ideas and issues explored in the text. It also influences the way the writer uses language.

Place

The stories in the 'Exploring Culture' unit are set all over the world. *Purple Hibiscus* is set in Nigeria, West Africa. *To Kill a Mockingbird* and *Of Mice and Men* are set in different parts of the USA, while *Mister Pip* takes place in Papua New Guinea.

These places are physically very different from each other as well as from Britain. Descriptions of the landscapes are important. They may include plants and trees that are unfamiliar (e.g. bougainvillea and hibiscus in *Purple Hibiscus*) or geographical features that dominate people's lives (e.g. the forest in *Mister Pip*). The weather, too, often has an influence on how people live their lives. In most of these texts it is much hotter than it is in Britain. What effect does this have on the characters and stories?

Modern Texts: Exploring Cultures

History and Politics

Societies change over time, so the time when texts are set can be important.

Purple Hibiscus is set against a background of political upheaval and violence. The events of the novel reflect the reality of Nigeria under military rule. There is a feeling that things are better now – both for the narrator personally and for the country. *Mister Pip* takes place against a background of civil war.

To Kill a Mockingbird is tinged with nostalgia as Scout recalls her childhood, but she is also aware of the racial tension and injustice that were rife in the southern states of the USA in the 1930s. The society she writes about is still heavily influenced by the aftermath of the American Civil War seventy years earlier. *Of Mice and Men* was written in the 1930s and reflects the life of many who were suffering because of the Depression.

If you are studying a text set in the past, it is important that you understand the history of the country or region where it is set.

Religion and Beliefs

Religion is central to many cultures and is an important element in many of these texts.

In *Purple Hibiscus* there is tension between the Catholic faith of the narrator's immediate family and her grandfather's traditional beliefs. Some characters are able to accommodate both traditions but others see them as being opposed.

Almost everyone in *To Kill a Mockingbird* professes to be Christian, and religion is an important part of their lives. However, black people and white people worship in different churches, and people interpret the Bible in different ways.

Traditions

Traditions are often, though not always, connected to religion. Religious rituals are often associated with the big events in people's lives, such as birth, marriage and death. Rituals surrounding death are described in *Purple Hibiscus*. Some rituals are part of the pattern of everyday life, like the Catholic and traditional prayers in *Purple Hibiscus*.

You may also come across examples of traditional art forms, traditional crafts, traditional dress and even traditional food and drink. All these things form part of a person's culture.

Language

English is spoken all over the world. In some countries it is the main or official language, whilst in other countries it is one of several languages.

When you look at the ways in which language is used in these texts, you should think about the following:

- Are any other languages apart from English spoken?
- Which characters speak in other languages? Why and what does it signify?
- When characters speak English is it Standard English?
- Do some of them, or all of them, speak in dialect?
- Which characters speak in dialect and why?
- How does the dialect differ from Standard English?

Helpful Hint

Do some research on the Internet to find out more about the culture of the place where your text is set. You could also look for articles about, or interviews with, the authors.

Modern Texts: Exploring Cultures

Close Reading

You will be asked in the exam to analyse and discuss a short passage (no more than a page) of your chosen text, before writing about the whole text.

By the time you take the exam you will be familiar with the text and you will probably have had a go at analysing some passages in detail. However, you will not have covered every single page of your text in the detail required for the exam. Don't worry, the examiners do not expect this. What they are looking for is a detailed 'exploratory' response to the text. They want to see how you respond to the passage in front of you.

So when you've read the passage, what sort of things should you comment on?

Language
- Is it entirely written in English? If not, when and why does the writer use other languages?
- Is any of it in dialect?
- When and why is dialect used?
- Are there any other unusual words or phrases, particularly ones that might be connected to the culture?
- Is there much descriptive language? Does the writer use adjectives and adverbs for effect?
- Is the diction at any point especially negative or positive?
- Does the writer use imagery, for example metaphors and similes? What difference does the imagery make?
- Is it written in the past or present tense?

Form and Structure
- Is it a first or third person narrative?
- Is the passage mainly or partly in the form of dialogue?
- Does it start in an effective way, grabbing your interest?
- Does the end of the passage make you want to read on? Why?
- How do things change during the course of the passage?
- Does the writer use varied sentence structures for effect, e.g. long sentences followed by short ones?
- Is there anything interesting or unusual about the use of punctuation?
- Is this passage a turning point in the plot?

Ideas, Themes and Settings
- What does the passage say about culture?
- Are there references to particular aspects of the culture?
- What other ideas, themes and issues are touched on?
- What is the attitude of the narrator to these ideas, themes and issues?
- Is the place important? Why?

Modern Texts: Exploring Cultures

Helpful Hints

It is essential that you comment on and analyse the details of the passage. You will need to make close reference to the text.

You should use a lot of very short quotations (just a few words). Make sure you show they are quotations by using inverted commas and remember **PEE:**
- **P**oint
- **E**vidence
- **E**xplanation

The Whole Text

The second part of the question in Section B picks up a theme or character from the selected passage. When you answer this part of the question, make sure you refer to the whole text and not the passage you have just been writing about.

The style of these questions is very similar to the style of questions used in Section A of the exam. But remember, you only have half the time.

In your answer you need to show that you understand and appreciate how the writer explores his or her ideas, themes and issues – particularly those connected to culture – and how he / she uses characters and settings.

Section B: Exam Tips

This exam is called **Unit 1: Exploring Modern Texts**. It is in two sections.

For Section B as for Section A, you are allowed to use unannotated texts. That means copies of your chosen texts that have no notes at all, whether on the text itself or on loose sheets.
- You may be given a 'clean' copy of the text in the exam room.
- You may be told to bring your own text. In this case, it is up to you to erase all notes from the book, whether made by you or by somebody else.

Before the exam, make sure that you have done everything for Section B that you have done for section A (see page 28).

In the exam, make sure that you do the following:
- Be aware of the time: you should spend **45 minutes** on Section B. It is helpful to spend about 5 minutes planning what you are going to write.
- Remember that there are two parts to the question. That means that you only have about **20 minutes** to write each answer.
- Quickly find the question on the text you have studied. There is only **one** question on each text in this section.
- Do not even think about reading the questions on texts you have not studied in class, however interesting the passages might look.
- Read the passage before you start answering. Make notes on it and highlight or underline key words and phrases.
- If there are bullet points (more likely in Foundation Tier questions) keep them in mind and make sure you cover all the points made in them.

On pages 36 and 37 you will find two sample questions. The first of these is a Foundation Tier style question and includes bullet points for the second part of the question. The second is a Higher Tier style question, without bullet points.

On pages 38 and 39 you will find partial answers to the first question with guidance on how to develop your answer.

If neither of the questions is about the text you have studied, pick a passage from your text and adapt the questions to suit it.

For guidance on 'key words' in exam questions see page 29.

Preparation Task

While you are re-reading your text, mark some key passages. Then try to make up questions to ask about them.

Exam Practice

Exam Practice

Answer this question in 45 minutes. When you have finished, ask a teacher or a fellow student to grade your answer.

Make sure you divide your time equally between the two parts.

Question 1
Chimamanda Ngozi Adichie: *Purple Hibiscus*

Read the passage below and then answer the questions.

a) How does Adichie use details in this passage to show attitudes towards traditional beliefs in Nigeria?

b) How are traditional beliefs presented in this story as a whole?
  - Write about the events described in the story.
  - Write about how Adichie shows different attitudes towards traditional beliefs.

'Look at this,' Papa-Nnukwu said. "This is a woman spirit, and the women mmuo are harmless. They do not even go near the big ones at the festival." The mmuo he pointed to was small; its carved wooden face had angular, pretty features and rouged lips. It stopped often to dance, wiggling this way and that, so the string of beads around its waist swayed and rippled. The crowds nearby cheered, and some people threw money toward it. Little boys – the followers of the mmuo who were playing music with metal ogenes and wooden ichakasa – picked up the crumpled naira notes. They had hardly passed us when Papa Nnukwu shouted, "Look away! Women cannot look at this one!"

The mmuo making its way down the road was surrounded by a few elderly men who rang a shrill bell as the mmuo walked. Its mask was a real, grimacing human skull with sunken eye sockets. A squirming tortoise was tied to its forehead. A snake and three dead chickens hung from its grass-covered body, swinging as the mmuo walked. The crowds near the road moved back quickly, fearfully. A few women turned and dashed into nearby compounds.

Aunty Ifeoma looked amused, but she turned her head away. "Don't look, girls. Let's humour your grandfather," she said in English. Amaka had already looked away, too, toward the crowd of people that pressed around the car. It was sinful, deferring to a heathen masquerade. But at the least I had looked at it very briefly, so maybe it would technically not be deferring to a heathen masquerade.

'That is our *agwonatumbe*,' Papa-Nnukwu said, proudly, after the mmuo had walked past. 'It is the most powerful mmuo in our parts, and all the neighbouring villages fear Abba because of it. At last year's Aro festival, *agwonatumbe* raised a staff and all the other mmuo turned and ran! They didn't even wait to see what would happen!'

Exam Practice

Answer this question in 45 minutes. When you have finished, ask a teacher or a fellow student to grade your answer.

Make sure you divide your time equally between the two parts.

Question 2
Harper Lee: *To Kill a Mockingbird*

Read the passage below and then answer the questions.

a) How does Lee use details in this passage to show racial tensions in the novel?

b) What is the significance of Calpurnia in the novel as a whole?

First Purchase African M.E. Church was in the Quarters outside the southern town limits, across the old sawmill tracks. It was an ancient paint-peeled frame building, the only church in Maycomb with a steeple and a bell, called First Purchase because it was paid for from the first earnings of freed slaves. Negroes worshipped in it on Sundays and white men gambled in it on weekdays.

The churchyard was brick-hard clay, as was the cemetery beside it. If someone died during a dry spell, the body was covered with chunks of ice until rain softened the earth. A few graves in the cemetery were marked with crumbling tombstones; newer ones were outlined with brightly coloured glass and broken Coca-Cola bottles. Lightning rods guarding some graves denoted dead who rested uneasily. It was a happy cemetery.

The warm bittersweet smell of clean Negro welcomed us as we entered the churchyard - Hearts of Love hairdressing mingled with asafoetida, snuff, Hoyt's Cologne, Brown's Mule, peppermint, and lilac talcum.

When they saw Jem and me with Calpurnia, the men stepped back and took off their hats; the women crossed their arms at their waists, weekday gestures of respectful attention. They parted and made a small pathway to the church door for us. Calpurnia walked between Jem and me, responding to the greetings of her brightly clad neighbours.

'What you up to, Miss Cal?' said a voice behind us.

Calpurnia's hands went to our shoulders and we stopped and looked around; standing in the path behind us was a tall Negro woman. Her weight was on one leg; she rested her left elbow in the curve of her hip, pointing at us with upturned palm. She was bullet-headed with strange almond-shaped eyes, straight nose, and an Indian-bow mouth. She seemed seven feet high.

I felt Calpurnia's hand dig into my shoulder. 'What you want, Lula?' she asked, in tones I had never heard her use. She spoke quietly, contemptuously.

Developing Your Answer

Look back at page 36 and remind yourself of the passage and the question on *Purple Hibiscus*.

You will see that you are asked to do two completely different things in the two parts of the question.

For part **(a)** you are asked to write about how Adichie uses details in this passage to show attitudes towards traditional beliefs.

The key word here is **details**. You should work your way through the passage picking up on words and phrases that show how the narrator and the other characters react to the traditional ritual they are watching.

The partial answer below gives an example of how you might structure your answer and some examples of how you can write about details.

Note that this does not cover all the relevant details in the passage. A real answer would be about twice as long. You might want to try expanding and improving on this answer.

A very brief introduction about the passage in context, saying where it comes in the story	The narrator, Kambili, and her brother have been staying with their parents in the family's second home in the village where the father was born. We already know that Kambili and her parents are Catholics, but that her grandfather (Papa Nnukwu) holds on to traditional beliefs, causing tension between him and his son. Here, Kambili's aunt has driven the children, her own children and Papa Nnukwu to see a traditional festival…
Use of PEE (Point Evidence Explanation). Notice that the quotations are very short and marked by inverted commas	The passage starts with Papa Nnukwu explaining what is happening to the children. It is clear that the narrator and her brother know very little about what is going on. Their grandfather talks about the 'mmuo', as if they are real spirits, not people dressed up and the writer chooses not to explain exactly what they are, so that the reader experiences them in the same way as Kambili does…
Paragraphs connected to help the essay 'flow' and 'signpost' each new point	The first mmuo is described as 'pretty' and 'wiggling this way and that', making her seem amusing and harmless, but there is a sudden change of mood at the end of the first paragraph, marked by Papa Nnukwu's excited shout…
Use of appropriate terms	In the next paragraph Adichie describes the mmuo in great detail. These details – the 'grimacing human skull', the 'squirming tortoise' and the dead chickens – make him sound repulsive and horrifying and associate him with death. The women's reaction to him contrasts with their reaction to the first mmuo…
Awareness of the importance of religion in the novel	Aunty Ifeoma's reaction is especially interesting. She tells the children to 'humour' their grandfather by looking away. It is significant that she speaks in English, so that her father cannot understand…
Reference to the way the writer uses language, focusing on its effect on the reader	Papa Nnukwu, on the other hand, clearly believes firmly in the spirits. He seems to really believe the women will be harmed if they look at the mmuo. He is also proud of his home village: 'all the neighbouring villages fear Abba'. Traditional beliefs, like loyalty to his village, are an essential part of his sense of identity…
	Kambili herself, however, is left confused by the experience. Her own religion tells her she should not take any part in this ritual and she feels she might have committed a sin by turning away…

Developing Your Answer

For part **(b)** of the questions you are asked to write about how attitudes towards traditional beliefs are presented in this story as a whole.

The key word is **whole**. Do not write about the passage again, but think about the whole story or novel.

The bullet points ask you to…
- write about the events described in the story
- write about how Adichie shows different attitudes towards traditional beliefs.

You have to make sure you cover both parts of the question. You need to think about the following:
- What people in the novel believe in and how they express these beliefs.
- Points in the story where traditional beliefs are discussed or rituals described.
- The attitude of various characters in the novel to traditional beliefs.
- The attitude of the narrator to these beliefs and their impact on her.

The writing frame below shows you how you might structure your answer to this part of the question.

Introduction. Clearly state what you are going to do. Refer back to the question.	In 'Purple Hibiscus' Chimamanda Ngozi Adichie writes about the relationship between Christianity and traditional beliefs in Nigerian society. She shows different attitudes towards traditional beliefs through her characters…
Mention the attitude to traditional beliefs that the narrator has been brought up with.	The narrator, Kambili, has been brought up as a Roman Catholic by her very strict father. He rejects the traditional beliefs of his childhood, which he calls 'pagan' and wants his children to have nothing to do with them…
Discuss Kambili's grandfather and describe some of his beliefs.	However, his own father, Papa Nnukwu, has refused to give up the old ways. When Kambili and her brother visit him…
Compare the attitudes of Papa Nnukwu and Eugene.	The two men represent two extremes. Papa Nnukwu blames the Catholic missionaries for everything that he sees wrong in his son, reacting to Christianity as violently as Eugene reacts to traditional religion…
Discuss the 'middle way' as shown by Aunty Ifeoma.	Adichie, however, shows that there is a middle way between the extremes. Aunty Ifeoma is a practising Catholic but, unlike her brother, embraces aspects of the traditional ways and believes it is important for her children to know about them…
Describe Papa Nnukwu's death and Father Amadi's reaction. Show the effect on Kambili.	When Papa Nnukwu is dying at Aunty Ifeoma's home, Kambili is surprised to see Father Amadi's attitude towards him…
Discuss Eugene's death and what it means in terms of the role of traditional beliefs.	Eugene's death demonstrates dramatically the result of ignoring tradition, his wife claiming that she has killed him with the help of 'a powerful witch doctor'…
Try to come to a conclusion about the role of traditional beliefs and the narrator's attitude to them.	While Adichie does not seem to be blaming either traditional or Christian beliefs for the family's troubles, she shows the dangers of intolerance and misunderstanding. Her narrator learns from the events of her childhood and by the end of the novel is beginning to establish her own identity…

Poetry

All students have to study poetry, and everybody will learn the same skills. However, there are two different options – being assessed by examination or being assessed by controlled assessment. Your teacher will have chosen which option to teach at the beginning of your course.

The next two pages explain how each of the two poetry units is organised.

The section which follows applies equally to Unit 2 and Unit 5.

All the examples given in this book are taken from poems in the AQA examination board's anthology, *Moon on the Tides*.

Unit 2: Poetry Across Time

There are two sections to the Unit 2 paper.

Section A
For Section A you are required to study a 'cluster' of fifteen poems from the anthology. There is a choice of four clusters, each based around a theme.

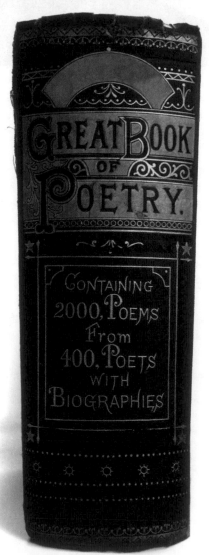

The themes are…
- character and voice
- place
- conflict
- relationships.

Each cluster includes poems by a range of poets. Some poems will have been written in the last few years and others several hundred years ago.

In the exam you will be given a choice of two questions on your chosen cluster. Each question will name one of the fifteen poems and you will be required to compare it to another poem from the cluster.

The style of the question will be slightly different depending on whether you are doing Foundation or Higher Tier.

When you write about the poems you will be expected to look at the following:
- **Ideas, themes and issues**: This means what the text is about, i.e. not the story but what it makes us think about.
- **Form, structure and language:** How the writer gets all these things across to the reader, using language, form and structure.

The examiners are looking for an **informed personal response.** That means they want to know what you think and feel about the poems.

Section B
For Section B there will only be one question, which all candidates must answer.

You will be given an 'unseen' poem. This means a poem that you have not studied and have probably never seen before.

There will be a different poem for Foundation and Higher Tier candidates and the question style will differ.

You cannot revise for this question in the same way that you will revise for Section A, but it will test the skills you have developed while studying the poems in the anthology. You should also have been given plenty of practice in discussing and writing about unseen poems. You may have practised with anthology poems taken from clusters other than the one you are studying.

As with Section A, the examiners want to see an informed, personal response. They want to know how you react to the poem in front of you, but they also want your response backed up by comment on…
- ideas, themes and issues
- form, structure and language.

Unit 5: Exploring Poetry

*N.B. If you take Unit 2, you will **not** take Unit 5.*

Unit 5 is assessed by means of controlled assessment.

You will be given a choice of a task and you will complete the task in school under the supervision of your teachers at a time chosen by them. This is most likely to be during normal lesson time, probably spread over several periods in order to give you three or four hours to complete the task. You will be given plenty of warning about when and where the assessment will take place.

You will have studied poems from the English, Irish or Welsh Literary Heritage and contemporary poems. Writers included in the 'Literary Heritage' are deceased writers with established reputations. Contemporary poets are poets who are still alive and writing now.

Many teachers will be using poems from the anthology, probably choosing a single cluster because this gives them a good range of poems which have already been linked by a theme. If you have not been using the anthology, your teacher will have made his / her own choice of poems.

For the task you will not have to write about all the poems you have studied, but you must write about both contemporary poems and poems from the Literary Heritage. You will also have to make links between the poems. If you are not sure whether a poem is from the Literary Heritage, check to see whether the poet's name appears on the list of 'approved authors' on page 95.

The task from which you will make your choice will be provided in advance. There will be one for each of the following topics:

- **Theme:** e.g. conflict, love, family, power.
- **Characterisation and voice**: e.g. relationships, heroes, female or male characters, comic characters.
- **Genre and form**: e.g. endings, importance of parts to whole, setting, conventions.

Whatever your task, you will be expected to be able to comment on ways in which the poets use language and form.

The assessors want to see that you understand how to look at a poem and write about it. They also want to see that you can make links between different poems. But, most importantly, they want to see your personal response to poetry.

What is Poetry?

> Prose = words in their best order;
> poetry = the *best* words in the best order.
>
> (Samuel Taylor Coleridge)

Thinking about the literature you have studied, what do you feel is the difference between poetry and prose?

Reading a Poem

When you read a poem for the first time, do not analyse it. Look at it, read it out loud, listen to it or do all three.

Respond to it instinctively. How does it make you feel? Does it make you sad or happy or angry, perhaps? Does it make you laugh? Do you identify with the feelings? Or does it leave you cold? There is no right or wrong way of responding to poetry. Your response is as valid as anyone else's.

Having read the poem a couple of times, you can start asking questions about it that might give you a greater understanding of what the poet is saying and how he / she is saying it.

Here are some suggestions:

1. What does the title tell you?
2. Who is speaking?
3. Who is being addressed?
4. Who is it about?
5. What do you think of the person or people it is about? What do you think the poet feels about them?
6. Where is it taking place?
7. When is it taking place?
8. What happens in the poem?
9. What does it look like on the page?
10. How is it arranged? Why do you think it is arranged in this way?
11. Does it rhyme? If so, can you identify a pattern?
12. What difference does the rhyme, or lack of rhyme, make?
13. Is there a regular rhythm or beat? Can you identify it?
14. What difference do the rhyme and rhythm make to the mood of the poem?
15. What would you say the mood is?
16. Is there anything interesting about the language the poet uses?
17. What does it sound like?
18. Does the poet use particular literary techniques such as alliteration, repetition or onomatopoeia? If so, what effect do they have?
19. Is there any interesting imagery, e.g. similes and metaphors?
20. What does the choice of imagery tell you about the poet's feelings?
21. What is the poem really about?
22. What is the poet's attitude to his / her subject?
23. Has the poet made his / her point successfully?
24. What do you think about the subject?
25. Does it remind you in any way of any other poems you have read?

That looks like a lot of questions – and you may think of even more. The following pages will look into these questions in more detail, as we consider…

- ideas, themes and issues
- character and voice
- form and structure
- language.

Poetry: Ideas, Themes and Issues

What are Ideas, Themes and Issues?

The poems in the anthology are arranged in 'clusters' according to theme:
- Character and voice
- Place
- Conflict
- Relationships

If you are taking Unit 2, you will only study one of these clusters, so you will already know what the connecting theme is in the poems you are studying. But it is not enough just to say a poem is 'about place' or 'about relationships'.

The themes are very broad and each cluster contains fifteen poems written over a long period of time by a wide variety of poets. You need to look at the following points:
- What aspects of the main theme the poet is writing about.
- What other ideas, themes and issues are present.
- What the poet's attitude is towards these ideas, themes and issues.
- How you can connect the poems through the treatment of ideas, themes and issues.

All these points apply equally if you are studying Unit 5, whether or not you are using the anthology.

How Ideas, Themes and Issues are Presented in Poetry

Once you have identified the main ideas, themes and issues in a text you need to consider how they are presented and what the poet might be saying about them.

Most poems are quite short and the poets do not have time to explore ideas, themes and issues in great depth or detail. More often they will concentrate on an incident or a moment in life – perhaps an anecdote or a kind of snapshot of someone's feelings at a given time.

Poems that tell a story include *My Last Duchess, Cold Knap Lake, The Charge of the Light Brigade* and *The Farmer's Bride.* Some poets, like Gillian Clarke in *Cold Knap Lake,* tell the story and then reflect on what it might mean. Other poems, like *My Last Duchess*, do not include the poet's thoughts directly, but let the readers make up their own minds about the meaning of the story.

Some poems do not have a story, but tell us directly about what the poet thinks or feels. Sometimes the poets express strong views about their subject, as in *Checking Out Me History*, *London* or *Sonnet 43*. Sometimes, like *Hawk Roosting* and *The Manhunt,* they work through description and imagery and leave the reader to infer the poet's attitudes and feelings.

It might be impossible for you to 'work out' what the poet's attitude to his / her subject is, because the poem is ambiguous. The poet either does not have an answer or is leaving it up to us, the readers, to come up with answers.

You should always remember that the same poem could mean very different things to different people. Your response and interpretation are as valid as anyone else's.

Poetry: Ideas, Themes and Issues

Try making some connections between the poems in your cluster.

Character and Voice

Why has the poet written about this person?

Which of the poems are about the following?
- Young people
- Men
- Fictional characters
- Historical characters
- Old people
- Women
- Mythical characters
- Outsiders

Which of them are written in the following way?
- The first person
- In the poet's own voice
- Using the voice of a persona
- The third person
- As a conversation

Which of them are about the following?
- Growing up
- Relationships
- Death
- Families
- Love
- Identity

What does the poet feel about the character?
- Love
- Amusement
- Fear
- Pity
- Admiration
- Disapproval

Relationships

Why has the poet written about his or her relationship?

What sort of relationship is it?
- Lovers
- Husbands and wives
- Brothers and sisters
- Friends
- Parents and children

What else is the poem about?
- Time passing
- Identity
- Death
- Betrayal
- Hope

What is the feeling of the poet or the voice he / she adopts towards the subject of the poem?
- Love
- Indifference
- Disgust
- Gratitude
- Obsession
- Hatred
- Admiration
- Anger
- Suspicion

And what is the attitude of the subject towards the poet / voice?

Conflict

Why has the poet written about conflict?

What kind of conflict is the poem about?
- A battle
- An argument
- A war that's happening now
- A fight
- A war a long time ago

Which of them are about the following?
- Power
- Loss
- The futility of war
- Relationships
- Death
- The horror of war
- The glory of war

What does the poet feel about the conflict?
- Sorrow
- Disgust
- Fear
- Anger
- Regret

Place

What does this place mean to the poet?

Which of the poems feature the following?
- A place in Britain
- A town or city
- Mountains / hills
- Water
- A place abroad
- The countryside
- Woods or forests

Which of them are about the following?
- Childhood
- Imagination
- Poverty
- How man relates to nature
- Memory
- Beauty
- Relationships

What does the poet feel about the place?
- Nostalgia
- Fear
- Dislike
- Awe
- Love
- Wonder

William Wordsworth said that poetry came from:

'emotion recollected in tranquillity'.

Having read the poems in your cluster, do you agree?

Poetry: Character and Voice

One of the four 'clusters' in the anthology is entitled **Character and Voice,** but whichever cluster or group of poems you have studied, it is an important aspect of the poems to think about.

When considering character and voice, you should think about the following:
- Who is speaking
- Who is being addressed
- Who is being described

Many poems are very personal. They express the thoughts and emotions of the person who wrote them. You will have noticed that the first person is used frequently in poetry. However the 'I' of the poem is not always the poet. Sometimes the poet adopts a **persona,** taking on a character and speaking in his / her voice.

The Poet

Unless you have reason to believe otherwise, it is usually safe to assume that the 'I' in a poem is the poet. However, the way the first person is used – even when it is clearly the poet – does change from poem to poem.

The poem might express the poet's inner thoughts and emotions, as if we have a window into his / her mind:

> I have looked upon those brilliant creatures
> And now my heart is sore
> (W.B. Yeats *The Wild Swans at Coole*)

We may get the sense that the poet is talking to us, perhaps explaining things, telling a story or putting across a point of view:

> We once watched a crowd
> pull a drowned child from the lake
> (Gillian Clarke *Cold Knap Lake*)

The poet could be 'in' the poem but as an observer, not the subject of the poem:

> As I made my way down Palestine Street
> I watched a funeral pass
> (Robert Minhinnick *The Yellow Palm*)

From all these poems we get a sense of the people who wrote them: their emotions, ideas, response to others and the questions that they are asking.

The Poet 'In Role'

Sometimes when a poem is in the first person, the speaker is clearly not the poet but a character that he / she has created. Such a character is often referred to as a **persona**. In this way, poets explore other people's minds and motives and allow them to put across their point of view. Usually the poet does not comment on or judge what the character is saying – that is left to the reader.

The anthology includes a wide range of characters speaking for themselves:
- Charlotte Mew speaks as the farmer in *The Farmer's Bride*: 'Three summers since I chose a bride'.

- Ted Hughes writes as a bird of prey in *Hawk Roosting*:

    > It took the whole of Creation
    > To produce my foot, my each feather:

- In *The Ruined Maid* Thomas Hardy takes on two roles – the girl from the country (his persona) and the 'ruined' girl whom she meets in town. Their conversation is, in effect, a mini drama.

Poetry: Character and Voice

The Person Being Addressed

Some poems contain not just 'I', but also 'you' (the second person). Sometimes the 'you' could be anyone – the person who happens to be reading the poem. Often it is a particular person to whom the poem is addressed and the focus of the poem is the poet's feelings for that person.

Quite a few poems in the anthology, especially in the **Relationships** section, are love poems and they give us an idea of the characters of both the poet and the person being addressed, as well as about the state of their relationship.

- Elizabeth Barrett Browning seems overwhelmed by the strength of her love: 'How do I love thee? Let me count the ways…' (*Sonnet 43*)

- Andrew Marvell is frustrated by the lady's lack of response to his attempts at seduction:

    Had we but world enough, and time,
    This coyness, Lady, were no crime,
    (*To His Coy Mistress*)

- Carol Ann Duffy sees her relationship as a duel with phones as weapons:

                    You've wounded me.
    Next time, you speak after the tone. I twirl the phone…' (*Quickdraw*)

However, the person addressed is not always a lover:
- Grace Nichols writes to her mother in *Praise Song for My Mother*.
- Robert Browning's persona in *My Last Duchess* addresses an envoy (messenger) from a count, whose daughter the Duke wants to marry.
- In *Sister Maude* by Christina Rossetti the speaker angrily addresses her sister.

Characters Described

Some poems focus on characters other than the narrator or the person being addressed.
- In *The Hunchback in the Park* Dylan Thomas barely features in the poem, instead concentrating on the strange figure he sees in the park:

    A solitary mister
    Propped between trees and water

- In Percy Bysshe Shelley's *Ozymandias* the poet re-tells a story that has been told to him by someone else:

    I met a traveller from an antique land
    Who said…

This might make the characters seem more distant from us. They do not speak for themselves. Therefore we, along with the poets, can speculate about who they are and what their thoughts and feelings might be.

Similarly, poems which focus on the poet or the persona might also describe other characters whose thoughts and feelings we are not privy to. For example:
- The father in Simon Armitage's *Harmonium*.
- The 'last Duchess' in Robert Browning's poem.
- The poet's son in Vernon Scannell's *Nettles*.

Preparation Task

Look briefly at the poems you have studied and see if you can answer the following questions about each one:
- Who is the speaker?
- Who is being addressed?
- Who is the main focus of the poem?
- What do we learn about the people in the poem?
- Why has the poet written about these people?

Poetry: Form and Structure

Structure and form are all about how poems are organised.

Some poems have very strict forms. They are **regular,** by which we mean they obey rules. These rules might be associated traditionally with a particular kind of poem, or might be rules the poets have given themselves to work within. Older poems are almost always regular, but some modern poets also like to work within strict forms.

Other poems seem to have no regular pattern. This sort of verse is sometimes called **free verse.**

Stanzas

The word stanza is Italian for 'room'. So if a poem is a house, the stanzas are the rooms within it. Stanzas are also referred to as **verses,** a word more often used when talking about songs.

One of the first things you will notice about a poem is whether it has more than one stanza. If it does, you should look at how many stanzas it has and if they are equal in length.

Here are some examples of poems that have stanzas of equal length:

- *Spellbound*: four stanzas of four lines each.
- *Wind*: six stanzas of four lines each.
- *The Wild Swans at Coole*: five stanzas of six lines each.

If you look at these poems you will see that they are all concerned with strong emotions and two of them with extreme weather. You might expect someone in the grip of strong emotion to be out of control, yet these poets organise their emotions in regular unchanging patterns. It could be that this helps them to understand their experiences. Do you think that the tension between the form and the content strengthens the impact on the reader?

Some poems are written in stanzas of slightly differing length:

- *Medusa* starts with a five-line stanza, but the other stanzas have six lines each.
- *Praise Song for My Mother* starts with three regular stanzas, but changes in the fourth.

Other poems have more complicated patterns. For example *Checking Out Me History* and *In Paris with You* have some stanzas of the same length but others that are different.

If stanza lengths vary, look at when and how the pattern changes. What is it that makes the poet at this point lengthen or shorten the stanza?

In any poem look at why a poet would start a new stanza at any given point. Is there a new idea being introduced? A new place? A new time?

Single Stanza Poems

The following poems have only one stanza:

- *Nettles*
- *The Falling Leaves*
- *Sonnet 116*

The obvious effect of this is that the poems seem to 'flow' more. *The Falling Leaves* could be divided into two parts, as the poet is reminded of the dead, but by not starting a new stanza, she emphasises how one thought flows into another. Also, in *Nettles* one thing is seen leading to another.

This is also the case in Shakespeare's *Sonnet 116*, but here the divisions within the poem are dictated by the **sonnet** form he is writing in: three sets of four lines (**quatrains**) followed by a couplet. With each new quatrain a new thought begins, and the couplet is used to finish the poem off neatly.

Poetry: Form and Structure

Rhyme

Rhyme can be an important feature of a poem. Although it is easy to spot, the effect it has is more difficult to put into words.

Rhymes can be used to emphasise certain words. They can make us laugh, but they can also help to hammer home a strong message or give a sense of order and calm.

As with songs, rhymes help us to remember a poem. Therefore, traditional forms of poetry, which were passed on orally, often feature strong rhymes.

The simplest way of rhyming is to rhyme one line with the next, forming a **rhyming couplet**. When children write poems this is what they usually do. So why do you think a poet like Thomas Hardy (in *The Ruined Maid*) would use rhyming couplets throughout his poem? And why would a modern poet like Simon Armitage do the same in *The Manhunt*?

Shakespeare often uses rhyming couplets to finish things off and make a memorable statement, as he does in *Sonnet 116*. Gillian Clarke also uses a single rhyming couplet to finish off *Cold Knap Lake*.

A traditional ballad usually has an *abab* rhyme scheme – rhyming the first line with the third and the second with the fourth. This pattern is used by many of the poets included in the anthology. Other poets use more complex or original rhyme schemes.

Look at the poems you have studied and see which ones use rhyme. If they do, is it a regular rhyme scheme or is there just the occasional rhyme? What effect do these rhymes have on your reading of the poem?

Rhythm

The rhythm of a poem comes from its pattern of stressed and unstressed sounds. If you read a poem out loud you will get a sense of the rhythm. Some poems have a regular rhythm. These rhythms can be very strong, for example in Tennyson's *The Charge of the Light Brigade*:

> **Half** a league **half** a league.
> **Half** a league **on**ward.

Here the stress is on the first syllable and it is followed by two unstressed syllables. This helps to give a sense of the pounding of the horses' hooves and the cannons.

One of the most common metres in poetry is the **iambic pentameter**. With a stress on every second syllable, this is sometimes said to resemble the human heartbeat. Wordsworth uses this technique in *The Prelude*:

> And, **as** I **rose** up**on** the **stroke**, my **boat**
> Went **heav**ing **through** the **wat**er **like** a **swan:**

The regular, quite gentle rhythm here adds to the mood of the poem. Hardy creates quite a different mood in *The Ruined Maid* by using only four stressed syllables per line and putting in extra, unstressed syllables:

> You **left** us in **tat**ters with**out** shoes or **socks**
> Tired of **dig**ging pot**at**oes, and **spud**ding up **docks;**

This is more like the rhythm of a nursery rhyme or traditional ballad and gives an upbeat, light-hearted feel to the poem.

Contemporary poets are less likely to employ strong rhythmical patterns as they generally prefer their poems to sound more like everyday speech; there are exceptions, for example in *Checking Out Me History*. Nevertheless, if you listen carefully, you will find that these poets still use rhythm and that the rhythm is an important part of creating the mood and tone of the poem.

Poetry: Language

According to the poet Coleridge, poetry is 'the best words in the *best* order'. When we looked at structure and form we were looking at the order the words were in. In the next few pages we will look at the words themselves.

Poets choose their words carefully. That choice is not just about the meanings of the words but also about what they sound like and what they might remind us of.

Diction

Diction refers to a writer's use of vocabulary.

Most of the poetry you have studied is written in Standard English. You might, however, notice some variations on Standard English.

If a poem does use a more colloquial form of English, perhaps using regional variations, think about why this might be:

- In *Hard Water* Jean Sprackland uses a couple of expressions that are common in the Midlands: 'Hey up me duck' and 'don't get mardy'. This helps to 'place' the poem in her childhood home and bring to life the people there.
- Grace Nichols, in *Price We Pay for the Sun*, uses the speech patterns of the West Indies, leaving out the verb 'to be', which gives a distinctive regional voice to the speaker:

> These islands
> not picture postcards

- In *Singh Song* Daljit Nagra changes the conventional spelling of words to reflect the distinctive accent of his speaker:

> I run one ov my daddy's shops
> From 9 o'clock to 9 o'clock
> And he vunt me not to hav a break
> But ven nobody in, I do di lock.

This has a comic effect but might also cause readers to question the stereotype of the man in 'di worst Indian shop / on di whole Indian road'.

- Gillian Clarke even uses words from languages other than English in *Neighbours*:

> glasnost
> golau glas
> a first break of blue.

She plays on the similarity of the Russian word *glasnost* (meaning openness) to the Welsh phrase *golau glas* (meaning blue light).

The poets' choice of vocabulary can also be influenced by the mood or atmosphere they want to convey.

In poems about war you would expect to find a lot of violent diction, but you will also find this kind of diction in poems on other subjects, for example 'slashed in fury' (*Nettles*) and 'tearing off heads' (*Hawk Roosting*).

In *The Manhunt* Simon Armitage, writing about a wounded soldier, combines military diction with medical diction:

> The parachute silk of his punctured wound.

In *Checking Out Me History* John Agard uses quite childish vocabulary as he recalls childhood lessons: 'Dem tell me bout de man who discover de balloon'.

A poet's choice of words can be dictated by the subject matter of the poem, but it is also influenced by his / her attitude to the subject and by the mood and atmosphere he / she wants to create.

Poetry: Language

Sound

It is important to comment on the way poets use the **sound** of words. To help you understand the importance of sounds, read the poems aloud or listen to someone else reading them. You may get the chance to hear some of the anthology poets reading their poetry at a live event. There are many recordings of poets reading their own work on the Internet, for example in The Poetry Archive's site.

The way a poem sounds is influenced by its rhythms and rhymes but also by the sound of the words themselves.

The most obvious way in which a sound reflects or adds to meaning is the use of **onomatopoeia**. This is when a word actually sounds like its meaning, for example:

- In *The Blackbird of Glanmore* by Seamus Heaney:

    The automatic lock
    Clunks shut...

This vividly conveys the sudden loud sound that makes the bird panic.

- Kathleen Jamie brings to life the sounds of water in *Crossing the Loch*: 'The oars' splash, creak and the spill'.

- In *The Falling Leaves* Margaret Postgate Cole uses both onomatopoeia and alliteration to imitate the sound of the wind: 'When no wind whirled them whistling to the sky'.

    The 'wh' sounds here almost make you whistle if you read the line aloud. The effect is strengthened by the poet's use of **alliteration**, starting a series of words with the same sound.

- Alliteration is also used to great effect by Ted Hughes in *Wind*:

                            ...a black-
        Back gull bent like an iron bar slowly.

- Tennyson uses 's' sounds in *The Charge of the Light Brigade*: 'Storm'd at with shot and shell'.

When you find examples of alliteration think about why the poet uses a particular sound. Some consonants, like 'd', 'k' and 'g' are hard. 'S' and 'f 'are softer, while 'p' and 'b' have an explosive quality. How does the repetition of the chosen consonant affect the overall mood of the poem?

If a poet uses a series of similar vowel sounds for effect it is called **assonance**. There is a very good example of this in D.H. Lawrence's *Storm in the Black Forest*:

    Now it is almost night, from the bronzey soft sky
    Jugfull after jugfull of pure white liquid fire, bright white
    Tipple over and spills down,

The poem moves from the heavy 'o' sounds of 'bronzey soft sky' to the short sharp sound of the 'i' 'liquid fire, bright white '. So from the still, heavy sky the lightning strikes and the atmosphere changes with the change in sound.

Many poets use **repetition** for effect, repeating not just sounds but whole words and phrases.

- In *Out of the Blue* Simon Armitage repeats several words, for example 'Waving, waving' and 'watching, watching'. This gives the impression not only of how actions are repeated but also of the weariness that this causes.
- In *Praise Song for My Mother*, by Grace Nichols, the repeated phrase at the beginning of each stanza makes it sound like a ritualistic chant or prayer.
- In *London* William Blake hammers his message home with his repetition of 'In every':

    In every cry of every Man
    In every Infant's cry of fear
    In every voice, in every ban

Poetry: Language

Imagery

An image is a picture and imagery refers to the way writers 'paint pictures' with their words.

Literal imagery is the description of things in order to convey a mood and atmosphere. More often when we refer to imagery in literature we mean **figurative imagery**, which is the use of an image or picture of one thing to tell us about another. The simplest form of figurative imagery is the **simile.** A simile makes a direct comparison between one thing and another, using a link word such as 'like', 'as' or 'than'.

- In Charlotte Mew's *The Farmer's Bride,* the farmer uses a series of similes to describe his bride:

    Shy as a leveret, swift as he,
    Straight and slight as a young larch tree,
    Sweet as the first wild violets, she.

    All the things he compares her to are things that he, as a farmer, would be familiar with. The similes make us see her as something wild and part of nature.

- In *Below the Green Corrie* Norman MacCaig compares nature to people:

    The mountains gathered round me
    Like bandits.

    This makes nature seem threatening and dangerous.

A **metaphor** is a comparison that is implied or hidden. Rather than saying one thing is like another thing, the writer describes it as being that thing:

- In *Quickdraw* Carol Ann Duffy uses a series of metaphors taken from cowboy films to describe a relationship:

    I twirl the phone,
    Then squeeze the trigger of my tongue, wide of the mark

    This helps to create a light-hearted tone, while showing the tension in the relationship.

- In *Praise Song for My Mother* Grace Nichols compares her mother to aspects of nature:

    You were
    sunrise to me
    rise and warm and streaming

    In this way she expresses the depth of the bond and the strength of her love.

- Vernon Scannell compares the nettles of his poem to soldiers:

    The regiment of spite behind the shed

    This makes them seem alive, with human attributes. This technique is called **personification.**

- In *Futility* Wilfred Owen personifies the sun:

    If anything will rouse him now
    The kind old sun will know:

Poets can also use personification to bring to life ideas or emotions.

- Andrew Marvell in *To His Coy Mistress* personifies time:

    But at my back I always hear
    Time's winged chariot hurrying near

Poets also use **symbols** to express ideas. A symbol is an object that represents a feeling or idea.

Some symbols are quite common, for example a lamb symbolising innocence. This idea is used by Gillian Clarke in *Neighbours*. The heart is often used to symbolise love. It is used in this way by Andrew Marvell in *To His Coy Mistress* and by Simon Armitage in *The Manhunt.*

Poets can also invent their own symbols. In *Harmonium*, for example, the musical instrument in the title becomes a symbol of the relationship between father and son. In *Cold Knap Lake* the lake symbolises memory and the past.

When you read a poem you should look for patterns in the imagery. What do the various images have in common and where do they come from? It is not enough to say that a poet uses a metaphor or a simile. You also need to say what the effect is of using that particular image.

Comparing Poems

Whether you are doing Unit 2 (exam) or Unit 5 (controlled assessment) you will be required to compare poems.

For the controlled assessment tasks you may be asked to compare several poems, but for the exam (Section A) you will only be asked to compare two poems. There will be a choice of two poems from the cluster you have studied.

If you are doing the Foundation Tier, the question will be in two parts:
- The first part will ask you to write about one named poem.
- The second part will ask you to compare the named poem to another.

For Higher Tier you will be given one question and you will have to compare the named poem with another of your choice throughout the answer.

Each question will focus on a particular aspect of the named poem and this will help you to choose an appropriate poem to compare it with. But whatever the question, you will need to compare the following:
- **Content:** what is happening in the poems.
- **Theme:** what aspects of the overall theme (character and voice; place; conflict; relationships) the poems are about.
- **Voice:** who is speaking.
- **Setting:** when and where the poems take place.
- **Structure and form:** similarities and differences between the way the poems are organised; the use made of rhyme and rhythm; how the structure relates to the poems' content.
- **Language**: similarities and differences in the use made of diction, sounds and imagery.
- **Attitude:** the different ways in which poets respond to their themes.
- **Your response.**

In deciding which poems to compare, you will probably choose poems that have a striking similarity, either in their themes or their style. For example, if you have studied **Conflict** you might choose to compare *Futility* to *Mametz Wood* because they are both set in the First World War. If you have studied **Character and Voice** you might choose to compare *The River God* to *Medusa* because both poems employ a 'persona'. Your choice will obviously depend on the focus of the question.

Once you have chosen the poems, remember you must look at both similarities and differences.

To help you revise, you could try picking out two poems from your cluster and filling in a chart like the one below.

	Similarities	Differences
Content		
Themes		
Voice		
Setting		
Structure and Form		
Language		
Imagery		
Attitude		
My Response		

The tables below and on the next page contain some suggestions for how you might link the poems in your cluster. You might also think of other connections.

Cluster 1: Character and Voice

Connection	Poems
Identity	*Checking Out Me History; Brendon Gallacher; Horse Whisperer*
Outsiders	*Give; The Ruined Maid; The Hunchback in the Park; On a Portrait of a Deaf Man; Singh Song; The Clown Punk*
Men	*The Hunchback in the Park; On a Portrait of a Deaf Man; Ozymandias; Singh Song; My Last Duchess*
Women	*The Ruined Maid; Medusa; My Last Duchess; Casehistory: Alison (head injury)*
Childhood	*Brendon Gallacher; Checking Out Me History; On a Portrait of a Deaf Man; The Hunchback in the Park*
Death	*On a Portrait of a Deaf Man; Casehistory: Alison (head injury); The River God; My Last Duchess*
Power	*Ozymandias; My Last Duchess; The River God; Medusa*
Using a persona	*Give; The Ruined Maid; Singh Song; My Last Duchess; The River God; Horse Whisperer*
Historical / Mythical characters	*Ozymandias; My Last Duchess; The River God; Medusa; Horse Whisperer*
Regional voices	*The Ruined Maid; Singh Song; Checking Out Me History; Brendon Gallacher*

Comparing Poems

Cluster 2: Place

Connection	Poems
Nature	*Neighbours*; *Below the Green Corrie*; *The Prelude*; *Spellbound*; *The Wild Swans at Coole*; *Storm in the Black Forest*; *Crossing the Loch*
Towns and cities	*A Vision*; *London*; *Hard Water*
Weather	*Spellbound*; *Storm in the Black Forest*; *Wind*; *Price We Pay for the Sun*
Water	*Cold Knap Lake*; *Crossing the Loch*; *Hard Water*; *The Wild Swans at Coole*; *The Prelude*
The Past / Memories	*Cold Knap Lake*; *The Blackbird of Glanmore*; *The Prelude*; *The Wild Swans at Coole*; *Below the Green Corrie*
Personification of nature	*The Moment*; *The Prelude*; *Below the Green Corrie*; *Wind*
The power of nature	*The Moment*; *Spellbound*; *The Prelude*; *Below the Green Corrie*; *Price We Pay for the Sun*; *Storm in the Black Forest*; *Wind*
Places where life is hard	*Neighbours*; *A Vision*; *London*; *Price We Pay for the Sun*
Death and mortality	*Neighbours*; *The Blackbird of Glanmore*; *London*; *Cold Knap Lake*
Symbolism	*The Wild Swans at Coole*; *The Blackbird of Glanmore*; *Cold Knap Lake*; *Hard Water*

Cluster 3: Conflict

Connection	Poems
The First World War	*Futility*; *Bayonet Charge*; *The Falling Leaves*; *Mametz Wood*
Recent conflicts	*Out of the Blue*; *The Yellow Palm*; *At the Border*; *Belfast Confetti*; *The Right Word*
People caught up in conflicts	*Belfast Confetti*; *The Right Word*; *At the Border*; *The Yellow Palm*; *Out of the Blue*
Soldiers	*Futility*; *The Charge of the Light Brigade*; *Bayonet Charge*; *Mametz Wood*; *Come On, Come Back*; *Poppies*
Death	*The Falling Leaves*; *Futility*; *Hawk Roosting*; *Come On, Come Back*; *Mametz Wood*; *The Charge of the Light Brigade*; *The Yellow Palm*
Power	*The Charge of the Light Brigade*; *Flag*; *Hawk Roosting*; *next to of course god america*; *Flag*
Nature	*The Falling Leaves*; *Hawk Roosting*; *Futility*; *Come On, Come Back*; *Poppies*
Fear / Escape	*The Right Word*; *Belfast Confetti*; *At the Border*; *Come On, Come Back*; *Out of the Blue*
Country / Patriotism	*next to of course god america*; *The Charge of the Light Brigade*; *At the Border*; *Flag*; *Poppies*
Imagery	*Belfast Confetti*; *The Falling Leaves*; *Futility*; *Mametz Wood*; *Poppies.*

Cluster 4: Relationships

Connection	Poems
Lovers	*The Manhunt*; *Hour*; *Quickdraw*; *Let me not unto the Marriage of True Minds (Sonnet 116)*; *How Do I Love Thee (Sonnet 43)*; *To His Coy Mistress*; *Ghazal*; *In Paris with You*
Families	*Nettles*; *Praise Song for My Mother*; *Harmonium*; *Sister Maude*; *Brothers*
Poems which use a persona	*The Manhunt*; *The Farmer's Bride*; *Sister Maude*
Natural imagery	*Ghazal*; *The Engine*; *Praise Song for My Mother*; *Let me not unto the Marriage of True Minds (Sonnet 116)*; *The Farmer's Bride*; *Nettles*
Other imagery	*Quickdraw*; *Harmonium*; *The Manhunt*
Time	*To His Coy Mistress*; *Born Yesterday*; *Nettles*; *Let me not unto the Marriage of True Minds (Sonnet 116)*; *Harmonium*
Unhappiness / Conflict	*In Paris with You*; *The Farmer's Bride*; *Sister Maude*; *To His Coy Mistress*; *Quickdraw*
Poems addressed to the subject	*Hour*; *Quickdraw*; *To His Coy Mistress*; *Born Yesterday*; *In Paris with You*; *Ghazal*; *Praise Song for My Mother*; *How Do I Love Thee (Sonnet 43)*; *Sister Maude*; *Brothers*
Poems written by men	*The Manhunt*; *In Paris with You*; *Harmonium*; *Let me not unto the Marriage of True Minds (Sonnet 116)*; *To His Coy Mistress*; *Nettles*; *Born Yesterday*; *Brothers*
Poems written by women	*Hour*; *Quickdraw*; *Ghazal*; *Praise Song for My Mother*; *How Do I Love Thee (Sonnet 43)*; *The Farmer's Bride*; *Sister Maude*

Exam Tips

The poetry exam is called **Unit 2: Poetry Across Time**. It is in two sections. For Section A…

- you will be given a 'clean' copy of the anthology
- you will not be allowed to take any other texts or additional notes in with you.

Before the exam make sure that you:

- Know all your poems well. You should read each one five or six times before the exam.
- Know the meaning of any unfamiliar words or phrases.
- Have read the notes you have taken or been given in class and that you understand them.
- Have come up with your own ideas about the texts – the examiner wants to know what you think, not what your teacher thinks.
- Have identified and put right errors that you know you make in punctuation, grammar and spelling.
- Have completed the exam preparation and exam practice tasks given in this section of the guide.
- Have perfected the PEE technique.
- Are able to write confidently about: ideas, themes and issues; character and voice; form and structure; language and technique.

In the exam, make sure that you:

- Are aware of the time: you should spend **45 minutes** on Section A. It is helpful to spend about 5 minutes planning what you are going to write.
- Quickly find the questions on the cluster you have studied.
- Read the two questions on your cluster carefully.

Choose one that you fully understand and you feel you can answer well.

- Use only the poems in the cluster you have studied.
- Annotate the poems you are using – underlining, highlighting and / or making brief notes on the anthology.

If you are doing **Foundation Tier:**

- Remember that your question is in two parts – effectively two short essays. Answer both parts.
- Divide your time equally between the two parts (20 minutes for each).
- For part (b) choose the second poem you are going to write on carefully. Make sure that it is the right poem for the question and that you can write confidently on it.
- Remember that in the first part of the question you only need to write about one poem, but it must be the poem named in the question.
- In the second part you must compare the named poem with a poem of your choice.

If you are doing **Higher Tier:**

- There is only one part to your question.
- Choose the second poem you are going to write about carefully. Make sure it fits the question and that you can write confidently on it.
- Make sure that you compare the two poems throughout the question. Do not write about one and then the other.

Exam Practice

In this exam the questions on the Foundation Tier and the Higher Tier exams are different in style. Make sure that you are aware of which tier you have been entered for.

Answer one of the following questions in 45 minutes. If none of them is about your text, try adapting the question. When you have finished, ask a teacher or a fellow student to grade your answer.

On pages 56–57 you will find…
- a writing frame for one of these questions, which will help you to understand how a good answer is organised
- a partial answer to another question.

Foundation Tier Questions

Question 1 Character and Voice

Answer both parts (a) and (b)

Part (a) What kind of person is speaking in *Singh Song*?

Part (b) Compare the ways in which writers present characters in this poem and one other poem.

Question 2 Place

Answer both parts (a) and (b)

Part (a) What are the poet's feelings about the place described in *A Vision*?

Part (b) Compare how the poets show their feelings about places in this poem and one other poem.

Question 3 Conflict

Answer both parts (a) and (b)

Part (a) What sort of conflict is shown in *Bayonet Charge*?

Part (b) Compare the ways in which conflict is presented in this poem and one other poem.

Question 4 Relationships

Answer both parts (a) and (b)

Part (a) What sort of relationship is shown in *Quickdraw*?

Part (b) Compare the ways that relationships are shown in this poem and one other poem.

Higher Tier Questions

Question 1 Character and Voice

Compare how the poets use a character's voice to express ideas in *Ozymandias* and one other poem.

Question 2 Place

Compare how poets write about the power of nature in *The Prelude* and one other poem.

Question 3 Conflict

Compare how poets show the effects of war in *Futility* and one other poem.

Question 4 Relationships

Different readers respond differently to poems. Compare your response to *Born Yesterday* with your response to one other poem.

Helpful Hints

Try to write about the poems that you enjoy and understand. You will have more to say about them and your enthusiasm will show in your answer.

On the following two pages you will find a writing frame for one of the questions above, which will give you an idea of how to structure an answer. You will also find a partial answer to another question with some key points highlighted.

Developing Your Answer

It is important when doing a comparison question that you compare the poems from the start and cover as many aspects of them as you can. The writing frame that follows gives you an idea of how you might structure an answer to the following Higher Tier question.

Question 2 Place

Compare how poets write about the power of nature in *The Prelude* and one other poem.

Introduction; making it clear which poems are being used	Both Wordsworth in 'The Prelude' and Emily Bronte in 'Spellbound' write about the experience of being alone surrounded by the wildness and power of nature…
Voice	Both poems are written in the first person and we can take it that the voice is the voice of the poet…
What is happening in the poems	However, while Wordsworth tells us a story from his boyhood and draws a lesson from it, Bronte simply tells us how she is feeling…
Form and structure	The extract from 'The Prelude' is part of a very long poem that traces Wordsworth's development as a poet…
	Bronte's poem, on the other hand, is short and self contained. It consists of three short stanzas…
Rhythm	The steady rhythm of 'The Prelude' is suited to the telling of a story….
	The rhythm of Bronte's poem is stronger, reflecting the harsh weather…
Language	Bronte uses alliteration and repetition…
Imagery	Although they both paint pictures of wild nature, Bronte simply describes what is going on around her…
	Wordsworth describes the landscape in detail but describes it as a living thing, using personification…
Attitudes to nature	The young Wordsworth seems to be overcome by the experience and rather frightened. He tries to escape the mountains…
	In contrast, Bronte is rooted to the spot. She 'cannot go'…
Conclusion referring back to question	Both poets are clearly in awe of the power of nature and they both seem attracted to it, however dangerous and frightening it might be. Wordsworth, however, wants to explain what it means to him…

Developing Your Answer

Here is an answer to part **(b)** of a Foundation Tier question. When you do part **(b)** you will already have written about the poem named in the question. Now you have to write about the similarities and differences between that poem and another poem of your choice.

Question 1 Character and Voice

Answer both parts (a) and (b)

Part (a) What kind of person is speaking in *Singh Song*?

Part (b) Compare the ways in which writers present characters in this poem and one other poem.

Both poems are mentioned

Correct terms are used to make points

Words used to indicate similarities

Words used to indicate differences

Quotations are used as part of PEE to support the points that are made

Like Daljit Nagra, Simon Armitage in 'Give' writes in the first person. Like Nagra, Armitage uses a 'persona', taking on the character of another person to get his points across. Both the shopkeeper in 'Singh Song' and the beggar in 'Give' might seem like outsiders in society, but they are very different characters.

First, they speak in very different ways. Nagra writes in the accent of his character: 'Ven I return vid my pinnie untied'. He changes the spelling of common words to reflect how the Indian man might sound. Armitage, on the other hand, writes in Standard English. However, the tone is still quite chatty as he talks directly to another person: 'Of all the doorways in the world/to choose to sleep, I've chosen yours'. We do not know who he is talking to – it could be someone he knows well, like an ex-girlfriend, or just any member of the public.

Just as Armitage could be talking to passers-by in the street, Nagra seems to be having conversations with the people who come into his shop.

Armitage's poem, like Nagra's, is arranged in stanzas, but his stanzas are shorter and more regular. This might make him seem more in control or more tense. The first and last stanzas have two lines and the middle two stanzas have three lines. Both poets use some rhyme and repetition, which help make the poems quite cheerful in their tone.

Like Nagra's character, the beggar does seem quite positive for most of the poem. When he speaks how he can 'swallow-swords' and 'escape from locks and chains' he sounds hopeful and entertaining, but he does these things for a price (copper; silver or gold) and he ends up begging just for enough for a cup of tea.

The characters in both these poems are the sort of people you might see in any street. Both poets use their voices to challenge stereotypes about them, but in the end there is a big difference between the two characters. While Nagra's character comes across as being happy with a positive outlook on life, at the end of the poem the beggar in 'Give' seems to be without hope: 'I'm on my knees'.

Unseen Poetry

Planning Your Answer

In the second part of the Unit 2 exam you will be given a poem you have never seen before and question(s) to answer on it.

By the time you get to the exam you should be confident about responding to and writing about poetry. All you need to do is to apply the approaches you have learned to the poem you are given.

When you see a poem for the first time, it is a good idea to read it through quickly once, before reading it more carefully and highlighting or underlining anything that strikes you as interesting, unusual or effective.

Have a look at the poem reproduced below and mark anything you think of interest.

> *The Eagle*
>
> He clasps the crag with crooked hands;
> Close to the sun in lonely lands,
> Ringed with the azure world he stands.
>
> The wrinkled sea beneath him crawls;
> He watches from his mountain walls,
> And like a thunderbolt he falls.
>
> Alfred, Lord Tennyson

Now consider the following aspects of the poem and jot down some answers to the questions.

The title:
- What does it make you think about?

Speakers / audience:
- Who is the speaker?
- Who is being addressed?

What happens:
- Is there a story? If so, what is it?

Settings:
- Where is it set?
- Does the place change?
- When is it set?
- Does the time change?

Form and structure:
- How is it arranged?
- Is there a regular rhythm?
- Does it rhyme?

Language:
- How does the poet use sounds?
- What sort of imagery is used?
- Is there anything else interesting about the language?

Themes, ideas and issues:
- What do you think the poem is really about?
- What is the poet's attitude to his theme?

Personal response:
- How does the poem make you feel and what do you think of it?

Unseen Poetry

Planning Your Answer

Here are some possible answers to the questions about *The Eagle*. Do you disagree with any of the answers, or is there anything you can add to them?

The title	What does it make you think about?	A bird of prey – something wild
Speakers / audience	Who is the speaker?	It is in the third person – the speaker is not in the poem
	Who is being addressed?	Nobody in particular or 'the reader'
What happens	Is there a story? If so, what is it?	The eagle watches for his prey. He swoops down to catch it.
Settings	Where is it set?	On a mountain or cliff above the sea – in the country
	Does the place change?	No.
	When is it set?	In the daytime.
	Does the time change?	No, it is set in a short space of time
Form and Structure	How is it arranged?	Two stanzas of three lines each.
	Is there a regular rhythm?	Yes. There is a strong regular rhythm, four stresses to each line.
	Does it rhyme?	Yes. In each stanza all three lines rhyme (rhyming triplets)
Language	How does the poet use sounds?	Alliteration of hard sounds ('clasps the crag')
	What sort of imagery is used?	The cliff is compared to a fortress. A simile compares the eagle to a thunderbolt. This gives a sense of power.
	Is there anything else interesting about the language?	Why is the sea described as 'wrinkled'? The use of the word 'falls' is unexpected.
Themes, ideas and issues	What do you think the poem is really about?	Power – the power of nature and maybe human power. Violence and beauty.
	What is the poet's attitude to his theme?	He does not comment but he seems to be in awe of the eagle and even admires him.
Personal response	How does the poem make you feel and what do you think of it?	I think it gives a good idea of what the eagle is like. It is short but makes a strong impression.

In the exam you will not have a list of questions and you are not expected to remember such lists yourself. This is just to remind you of some of the things you might consider when looking at a poem and to help you with your preparation for the exam.

When you write the answer, make sure that you explain the effect of any techniques you mention.

You are not expected to cover every aspect of the poem and you are certainly not expected to understand everything about it on a first reading. On the other hand, you might come up with ideas that nobody else does. The most important thing is that you respond to what you see in front of you.

You will be given one question, which may focus on a particular aspect of the poem. Make sure you answer the question you are given.

Unseen Poetry: Exam Practice

Developing Your Answer

Here is an example of the type of question you might get in the exam, with an annotated model answer.

The Eagle (see page 59 for text)

Question: What do you think the poet is saying about the eagle, and nature in general, and how does he present his ideas?

Answer:

In this poem the poet writes about an eagle, who is looking down at the land and sea, waiting for his prey.

The poem is very short but powerful. It has two stanzas of three lines each. In the first the eagle stands on the mountain. In the second he sees something beneath and 'falls'.

The focus is on the eagle. He seems to be the only living creature in the landscape. The eagle is in command of his surroundings. He is fierce and possessive. He 'clasps' the crag, as if it belongs to him. The alliteration of the hard sounds in 'clasps the crag with crooked hands' adds to the sense of violence.

The eagle is personified and made to sound like a human being. Right at the start he is referred to as 'he' rather than 'it' and he is said to have 'hands', not claws as you would expect. The use of the word 'lonely' is also interesting. Although it refers to the lands, it implies that the eagle himself is lonely, perhaps saying something about the loneliness of the powerful.

The poet's imagery makes the eagle sound like a king or general. The mountain is described as being like a castle: 'mountain walls'. His height, 'close to the sun', also implies power. It reminds me of the story of Icarus (who flew too high and, because the sun melted the wax in his wings, fell to the earth).

When he swoops, it must be to attack an animal, although the poet does not say so. Here he is compared to a thunderbolt, which is powerful and violent. The ending is very sudden and mirrors the suddenness of the eagle's attack.

The poem has a strong regular rhythm of four beats a line. The strength of the beat reflects the strength of the eagle. All three lines in each stanza rhyme, which is unusual. You might expect a fourth line. Having just three reflects the quickness of his actions.

The eagle is part of nature; the crag, the sun, 'the azure sky' and the sea are all described. He is part of its beauty but he also represents its power. The poet seems to be impressed not just by the beauty of nature but also by its power and violence.

Brief introduction, mentioning the subject of the poem

The structure and content of the poem

Language techniques and their effect discussed

Personal response and interpretation

Form and structure discussed

Effective conclusion, discussing the poet's attitude and focusing on the question.

The answer above focuses on the question and discusses the poet's language, form and structure, and themes, ideas and issues. The PEE technique is used throughout, with plenty of short quotations from the text.

It is clear from the essay that the student has learned to appreciate and understand poetry, but it is also a personal response.

Unseen Poetry: Exam Practice

The most useful way to revise for the 'unseen poetry' part of the exam is to read and think about poetry and perhaps attempt some practice answers. On this page there is a poem with questions in the style of the Foundation Tier and another one with a Higher Tier style question.

On page 62 you will find essay plans for both questions. You might want to add to the plan before trying to answer the question in essay form.

Foundation Tier

Read the poem below and answer the questions that follow.

The Little Boy Lost

"Father, father, where are you going?
  Oh do not walk so fast!
Speak, father, speak to your little boy,
  Or else I shall be lost."

The night was dark, no father was there,
  The child was wet with dew;
The mire was deep, and the child did weep,
  And away the vapour flew.

William Blake

1 What is the speaker saying about the little boy and his feelings about his father?

And

2 How does the poet present the boy and his feelings through the ways in which he describes them?

Higher Tier

Read the poem below and answer the question that follows.

Chidiock Titchborne's Elegy

My prime of youth is but a frost of cares,
  My feast of joy is but a dish of pain,
My crop of corn is but a field of tares,
  And all my good is but vain hope of gain.
    The day is past, and yet I saw no sun,
    And now I live, and now my life is done.

My tale was heard and yet it was not told,
  My fruit is fallen and yet my leaves are green;
My youth is spent and yet I am not old,
  I saw the world and yet I was not seen.
    My thread is cut and yet it is not spun,
    And now I live, and now my life is done.

I sought my death and found it in my womb,
  I looked for life and saw it was a shade;
I trod the earth and knew it was my tomb,
  And now I die, and now I was but made.
    My glass is full, and now my glass is run,
    And now I live, and now my life is done.

1 Tichborne wrote this poem in the Tower of London the day before his execution. What do you think he is saying about his life and death and how does he present his ideas?

Unseen Poetry: Planning Your Answer

Foundation Tier: *The Little Boy Lost*

1 What is the speaker saying about the little boy and his feelings about his father?

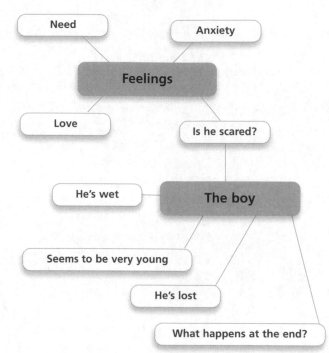

- Need
- Anxiety
- **Feelings**
- Love
- Is he scared?
- He's wet
- **The boy**
- Seems to be very young
- He's lost
- What happens at the end?

2 How does the poet present the boy and his feelings through the ways in which he describes them?

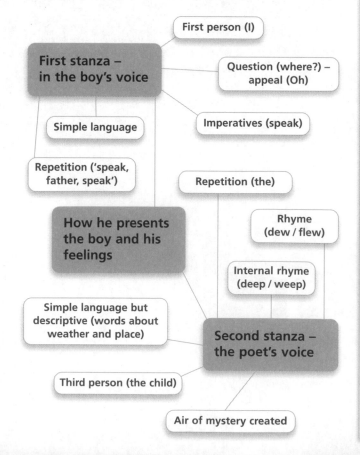

- First person (I)
- **First stanza – in the boy's voice**
- Question (where?) – appeal (Oh)
- Simple language
- Imperatives (speak)
- Repetition ('speak, father, speak')
- Repetition (the)
- **How he presents the boy and his feelings**
- Rhyme (dew / flew)
- Internal rhyme (deep / weep)
- Simple language but descriptive (words about weather and place)
- **Second stanza – the poet's voice**
- Third person (the child)
- Air of mystery created

Higher Tier: *Tichborne's Elegy*

Tichborne wrote this poem in the Tower of London the day before his execution. What do you think he is saying about his life and death and how does he present his ideas?

- First person – very personal and reflective.
- He's young but he knows he is going to die.
- There is a central paradox – he is young, healthy and alive but he knows he will die. This is expressed in the imagery: a useless crop; a day with no sun; autumn in summer.
- Three stanzas
- Very regular
- Iambic pentameters – heartbeat?
- First four lines of each stanza rhyme *abab*. Next two form a couplet.
- What's the effect of the regularity?
- The last line of each stanza is the same (a refrain) – underlines that death is inevitable.
- Heavy rhymes with 'done' give a sense of finality.
- Repetition of 'my' and 'I' stress the personal nature of the poem.
- How does he feel about his life?
- How is he approaching death? – seems to be resigned to it.
- Does it make a difference knowing when it was written?
- It's very moving – not just about him but about anyone who has to think about death.

Preparation Task

Is there anything you would add to the plans above? Is there anything you would disagree with? Try writing a complete answer based on one of the plans.

Helpful Hint

Remember that in the exam you only have a very short time to complete this question. Whatever form your plan is in, make it quick. It does not matter how rough or sketchy it is. It is for your benefit, not the examiner's.

Read the poem below. Then answer either the Foundation Tier or the Higher Tier question on it.

Do Not Go Gentle Into That Good Night

Do not go gentle into that good night,
Old age should burn and rave at close of day;
Rage, rage against the dying of the light.

Though wise men at their end know dark is right,
Because their words had forked no lightning they
Do not go gentle into that good night,

Good men, the last wave by, crying how bright
Their frail deeds might have dance in a green bay,
Rage, rage against the dying of the light.

Wild men who caught and sang the sun in flight,
And learn, too late, they grieved it on its way,
Do not go gentle into that good night.

Grave men, near death, who see with blinding sight
Blind eyes could blaze like meteors and be gay,
Rage, rage against the dying of the light.

And you, my father, there on that sad height,
Curse, bless, me now with your fierce tears, I pray.
Do not go gentle into that good night.
Rage, rage against the dying of the light.

Dylan Thomas

Foundation Tier Question

1 What do you think the poet feels about his father's death in the poem?

And

2 How does the poet present his feelings about death?

Higher Tier Question

1 What do you think the poet is saying about attitudes to death, and how does he present his ideas?

You might want to do a quick plan in the space opposite before writing your answer in full.

Try not to take more than **30 minutes**. After you have completed the question, you could show it to a teacher or fellow student and ask for their comments and advice.

Writing Plan

Poetry: Approaching Unit 5

*N.B. If you are sitting the Unit 2 exam, you will **not** take Unit 5.*

Tips for the Controlled Assessment

The poetry unit for controlled assessment is called **Unit 5: Exploring Poetry.**

You will be given one task, which asks you to make links between a range of poems.

- You must use both contemporary poems and poems from the English Literary Heritage.
- You may use poems from the AQA anthology, but you do not have to.
- You are allowed clean, unannotated copies of the texts you are writing about.

- You are allowed brief notes
- You are not allowed to take any other texts, draft essays or detailed plans in with you.
- You are allowed access to a dictionary and thesaurus and to grammar and spell check programmes.
- You will be given between three and four hours to complete the task under supervision.
- The word limit is 2000 words

Before the controlled assessment make sure that you:
- Know exactly when and where it will take place.
- Know all your poems well. You should read each one five or six times before the assessment.
- Choose the question you are going to answer and the poems you are going to write about.
- Thoroughly understand the question.
- Have read the notes you have taken or been given in class and that you understand them.
- Have planned what you are going to write and possibly done a preliminary draft.
- Have kept a record of any sources you have used, for example published notes and websites.
- Have practised writing in the form required.
- Have come up with your own ideas about the texts – the examiner wants to know what you think, not what your teacher thinks.
- Have perfected the PEE technique.

During the controlled assessment make sure that you:
- Are aware of the time: you will be given between three and four hours to complete your work. Be absolutely clear about how long you have and how the time is divided up (it is quite likely it will be spread over three or four one-hour lessons).
- Divide the time well. You may be answering one or two questions.
- Read your questions carefully to remind yourself of what you are being asked to do.
- Find your texts quickly. Annotate them, underlining, highlighting and / or making brief notes.
- Quickly jot down your plan.
- If you have time and think it is useful, do a first draft. Remember that all drafts and plans must be handed in with your completed work.
- Do not ask your teacher or any of your fellow pupils for help.
- Check all your work carefully for errors in spelling, punctuation and grammar.

All students have to study…
- one play by William Shakespeare
- a text from what is known as the English Literary Heritage.

Everybody will learn the same skills, but there are two assessment options:
- Assessment by exam.
- Assessment by controlled assessment.

Your teacher will have chosen which option to teach at the beginning of your course.

Unit 3: The Significance of Shakespeare and the English Literary Heritage

Unit 3 is assessed by means of **controlled assessment.**

You will be given a choice of a task to do and you will complete the task in school under the supervision of your teachers at a time chosen by them. This is most likely to be during normal lesson time, probably spread over several periods, in order to give you three or four hours to complete the task. You will be given plenty of warning about when and where the assessment will take place.

You will have studied one Shakespeare play and one other text from the English Literary Heritage. On page 95 there is a list of authors whose work can be used.

In the task you will write about both texts you have studied and they will be linked in the question, but you do not need to compare them.

The task from which you will make your choice will be provided in advance. There will be one for each of the following topics:
- **Theme and ideas:** e.g. conflict, love, family, power.
- **Characterisation and voice:** e.g. relationships, heroes, male or female characters, comic characters.

Whatever your task, you will be expected to be able to comment on the social and historical context of your texts.

Unit 4: Approaching Shakespeare and the English Literary Heritage

Unit 4 is assessed by **examination**. There are two parts to the exam – Section A and Section B.

For both Sections A and B you will be expected to look at the following:
- Ideas, themes and issues
- Characterisation
- Settings
- The writers' language and techniques.

The examiners are looking for an **informed personal response**. That means they want to know what you think and feel about the poems.

Section A
For Section A you are required to study **one** of the following plays by Shakespeare:
- *Macbeth*
- *Romeo and Juliet*
- *Much Ado About Nothing*
- *Twelfth Night*
- *Julius Caesar*

In the exam you will be given a choice of two questions on your chosen play. You will be given an extract from your play and asked to write about it and another part of the play.

Section B
For Section B you will study **one** of the following texts:
- *Pride and Prejudice* by Jane Austen
- *Wuthering Heights* by Emily Bronte
- *Great Expectations* by Charles Dickens
- *The Withered Arm and Other Wessex Tales* by Thomas Hardy
- *Animal Farm* by George Orwell

In the exam you will be given a choice of two questions on your chosen text.

Shakespeare: Ideas, Themes and Issues

When you look at ideas, themes and issues in Shakespeare's plays, think about what matters to the writer, as shown through the story and characters. What is Shakespeare trying to say to the audience? What does the text make you think about?

You also need to think about what the world was like when Shakespeare was writing and what it might have been like for his characters. How were people expected to behave? How did they act towards each other? What did they believe?

Try to identify at least five themes or ideas that are important in your text. For example, you could write five sentences similar to the following:

- *Macbeth* is about ambition.
- *Romeo and Juliet* is about parents and children.
- *Much Ado About Nothing* is about misunderstandings.
- *Twelfth Night* is about love.
- *Julius Caesar* is about power.

You may find that the themes identified above are present in more than one Shakespearean play. Throughout his long career, Shakespeare kept returning to the same ideas but looking at them in different ways and forming different viewpoints.

The spider diagram below shows some of the ideas, themes and issues that appear frequently in Shakespeare's plays. Some occur more frequently in tragedies, like *Macbeth, Romeo and Juliet* and *Julius Caesar,* while others are more likely to appear in comedies, like *Twelfth Night* and *Much Ado About Nothing.* Think carefully about each of these themes or ideas before deciding whether or not it is explored in your text. Then write a sentence or two about why you think it is present.

For example:

- I think ambition is an important theme in *Julius Caesar* because Caesar is killed when he achieves his ambition to rule Rome alone. The conspirators also have ambitions and these ambitions divide them.
- Jealousy is important in *Much Ado About Nothing* because the plot against Hero is the result of Don John's jealousy of his brother's friendship with Claudio.
- In my opinion one of the most important themes in *Macbeth* is order and chaos. By killing Duncan, Macbeth upsets the proper order of things and Scotland descends into chaos.
- The idea of rebirth is very important in *Twelfth Night* because Viola thinks her brother is dead and his reappearance brings hope and a new beginning.
- Friendship is an important part of *Romeo and Juliet.* It is because of his friendship with Mercutio that Romeo kills Tybalt.

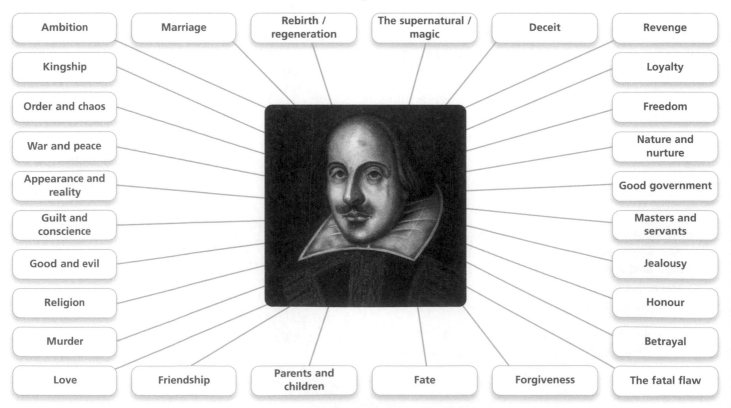

Shakespeare: Ideas, Themes and Issues

How Ideas, Themes and Issues are Presented in Shakespeare

Shakespeare does not have a 'voice' through which to express his ideas and opinions, so we never know what he really thought about the themes, ideas and issues that we see in his plays. However, that has not stopped thousands of people during the last four hundred years talking and writing about what they think Shakespeare meant. It is a measure of how good his plays are that there have been so many different interpretations. Everyone who sees or reads a Shakespearean play will have his / her own opinion about what is going on.

Ideas, themes and issues are presented to us through dialogue and action. The theatre is a visual medium and images can be much more powerful than words. The sight of Banquo's ghost, unseen by everyone except Macbeth and the audience, speaks volumes about betrayal and guilt.

When Juliet appears on the balcony above Romeo, the audience sees the goddess that he sees and understands his love. And when Sebastian turns up in *Twelfth Night* and is confronted by his mirror image in Viola, the theme of 'appearance and reality', as well as the bond between brother and sister, is summed up in a moment before our eyes.

Through dialogue, Shakespeare can give us more than one viewpoint or angle on a particular subject. Different characters have different ideas. Brutus and Cassius in *Julius Caesar* have several debates about what they should do or should have done.

Brutus is an idealist and Cassius a pragmatist. Brutus bases his decisions on a strong moral code, while Cassius thinks about what will be advantageous to him. Which one we agree with may depend on what we already know of their characters and whose side we would be on if they were real people. We might, however, decide that they both have a point.

In Shakespeare we constantly see characters making decisions and the consequences of those decisions. Many people are shocked by the Nurse telling Juliet to forget about Romeo and marry Paris. According to the characters' (and probably most of the audience's) moral code, it is clearly wrong.

However, if Juliet had followed this advice, she and Romeo might well have lived and been happy. As it turns out, they do something far worse in the eyes of many, by killing themselves.

Quite often in Shakespeare a character will speak his / her thoughts directly to the audience, in a **soliloquy** or **aside.** A soliloquy tells us what the character is actually thinking. When Macbeth shares with us his doubts about killing Duncan, he weighs up the issues involved. Through him we get to understand the issues of kingship, loyalty and ambition.

Every member of every audience reacts differently to what happens in a Shakespearean play. We can be influenced by directors' and actors' ideas about the play, but in the end we have to make up our own minds. Shakespeare asks more questions than he gives answers.

If you take into account different possible answers to the questions he and you ask, you are more likely to do well in your Shakespeare unit.

Shakespeare: Characters

It is quite likely that one of the questions on your play will focus on a character.

You will be given a short extract from the play and you will be asked to write about what a character is thinking and feeling at that point in the play and how the character is presented.

You will then be asked to write about the same character at a different point in the play.

When you tackle this sort of question you need to bear in mind everything you have learned about the character up to that point in the play, for example:

- Background
- Personality
- Relationships with other characters
- Motivation

We usually learn quite a lot about the main characters in the first act. Make a list of all the characters in your play that you think you might be asked about. Then try making brief notes about each one under the headings above.

The following example is about the main characters in *Much Ado About Nothing*. If you have studied *Much Ado About Nothing* see if you can add to the grid. If you have studied another play, make your own grid for your characters (see below).

It is very important to think about how the characters change during the play. They certainly find themselves in different situations at the end of the play – whether married, like Benedick and Beatrice, or dead like Macbeth – but how did they get there, and how did their experiences change them?

You might want to trace a character's development, pinpointing the events that influence him / her. Use the example below (about Macbeth) as a model:

What Happens?	What Effect Does It Have?
He meets the witches for the first time	He starts to think about his future and becomes ambitious to be king.
He kills Duncan	He becomes king – he is now powerful and he turns against his friend, Banquo, to protect his position.
He sees Banquo's ghost	He feels guilty and acts strangely.
He visits the witches	He feels very insecure and is frightened of losing his crown, but this makes him even more ruthless.
Macduff and Malcolm invade Scotland	Thinking he is invincible, he becomes defiant and brave.

Character	Background	Personality	Relationships	Motivation
Benedick	He is an old soldier and has never married.	He is witty and quite rude. He is loyal and brave.	He is a trusted friend of the Prince and close to Claudio. He has known Beatrice for a long time.	He wants to carry on as he is, enjoy himself and avoid marriage.
Beatrice	She is an orphan and depends on her uncle. She is not married.	She is very witty and playful. She can be hot-headed but is loyal to her friends.	She is very close to Hero. She has known Benedick a long time and may have been in love with him.	.
Claudio	He is a young soldier, who has done well in the war.	He falls in love quickly, but is easily influenced.		
Hero	She is the only daughter of Leonato, the Governor of Messina.			
Don John				He wants revenge. He is jealous of Claudio.

How Characters are Presented

What They Say

If Shakespeare wants us to know what his characters are really thinking and feeling, they speak directly to us, the audience. A long speech to the audience is called a **soliloquy.** When a character turns briefly to the audience to comment on something happening on stage, it is called an **aside.**

If a character speaks directly to us, we know he / she is telling the truth. We share the character's thought processes.

We know Macbeth has a conscience when he puts forward the arguments against killing Duncan. On the other hand, when Lady Macbeth is alone she does not express any self doubt.

However, Shakespeare's characters do not always tell the truth when they speak to others. All five set plays contain characters who lie, cheat and deceive, for example Don John in *Much Ado About Nothing* and Sir Toby Belch in *Twelfth Night*.

We do not have to guess who is telling the truth and who is not. Shakespeare makes it clear whether characters can be trusted or not; for example, a character may have discussed his or her plans in a previous scene.

Before she welcomes Duncan into her house, Lady Macbeth tells her husband to 'look like the innocent flower/but be the serpent under't' (Act 1 scene 6). Some characters may tell others about their lies afterwards, as when (in *Much Ado About Nothing*) Borachio explains to Conrade that the plot against Hero was planned by 'the devil, my master' (Act 3 scene 3).

What Other Characters Say About Them and to Them

Sometimes there is a consensus of opinion about a character. At the beginning of *Macbeth* everyone is full of praise for Macbeth's bravery and loyalty. Yet by the end of the play he has been called 'tyrant', 'devil' and 'fiend'.

At other times, you need to think about who the speaker is. In *Julius Caesar* we can believe that Brutus is 'the noblest Roman of them all' (Act 5 scene 5) because the words are spoken by Antony, his enemy. We might be less inclined to trust the opinion of the citizens as their loyalties shift from Caesar to the conspirators and then to Antony.

Just as they have different views on ideas and issues, characters have differing views about other characters. In *Romeo and Juliet* the Nurse and Lady Capulet are both fans of Tybalt, unlike almost everybody else. You might be able to see both points of view.

How They Act and React

The main way in which we learn about characters is through their actions.

When Lady Macbeth walks in her sleep and washes her hands repeatedly, we know her conscience has finally caught up with her. In *Much Ado About Nothing* when Hero says nothing in response to Claudio's accusations and then faints, we can see that she is innocent.

Their reactions to events, too, tell us a lot about what sort of people they are and how their characters are developing.

Macduff's reaction to the news of his wife and children's murders is very moving and tells us what kind of man he is. Capulet's reaction when he thinks Juliet is dead is in stark contrast to his earlier treatment of her. Benedick's reaction to Beatrice's command to 'kill Claudio' tells us not only about his sense of honour, but also about his growing feelings for Beatrice.

Shakespeare: Settings

When you are revising a Shakespearean play, it is important to think about its setting. This means both when and where the play is set. You also need to think about the context in which Shakespeare was writing.

Shakespeare has remained popular for four hundred years because we can still relate to his characters and their concerns. However, you may not always completely understand the assumptions, beliefs and manners shown in his plays.

Elizabethan and Jacobean audiences would certainly have had no trouble understanding the many references to religion in his plays, as at that time England was an overwhelmingly Christian country.

Although there were differences between Christians, everyone would have recognised the biblical references. Yet, at the same time many people believed strongly in astrology, even though the Church disapproved of this.

Certain moral values, too, were common to most people. For example, chastity was much more highly prized than it is in today's society. This is evident in *Romeo and Juliet* and *Much Ado About Nothing*.

Many people also believed that the social order, with the King or Queen at the top, was derived from God and should not be tampered with. Similarly, the authority of parents over children might be seen as sacred. However, these assumptions are often challenged in Shakespearean plays.

Shakespeare set his plays in a variety of places and times, often drawing on existing stories. Each set text reflects not just the age in which it was written but also Shakespeare's ideas about the place and time in which he chose to set it.

Place is just as important as time. Shakespeare's theatres did not use naturalistic sets / scenery to reproduce different places. If it had, he would not have been able to take us so quickly from one scene to another.

Instead, he sketches in each new scene with a few words of dialogue.

Romeo and Juliet

The story of *Romeo and Juliet* was very popular before Shakespeare wrote his play. Shakespeare kept its setting in Verona, a city in Italy.

Although many of the ideas and attitudes in the play would still have existed in Shakespeare's England – for example, the idea that a man could choose a husband for his daughter – many in his audience might have felt them old-fashioned and more suited to the Italy of a few hundred years earlier.

Italy certainly seems an appropriate setting for the play. During the Renaissance quite small cities like Verona operated as independent states, often ruled by princes. Feuds between rich families were not uncommon. The Catholic faith was an important part of everybody's life. Italy was also the origin of many love stories and the place where the sonnet was invented: Italian literature was very popular in England.

The play takes place over a few days. Time and place are both important in creating mood and atmosphere. In the hot dusty streets at noon it seems inevitable that young men will turn to violence. In Capulet's house, the excitement of a masked ball provides the ideal setting for two strangers to fall in love. The coolness of the orchard at night briefly provides a private place for the exchange of vows. Friar Lawrence's cell is a place to which both Romeo and Juliet can escape. And the great tomb of the Capulets is a suitably macabre setting for the final act of the tragedy.

Much Ado About Nothing

Much Ado About Nothing is set in Messina, a town in Sicily. Although the characters are supposed to be Italians and Spaniards, in most respects they behave just as English people of Shakespeare's day might have been expected to behave. The war of words between Benedick and Beatrice reflects the Elizabethan fashion for playing with words, and the comical 'watch' might have come straight from Shakespeare's home town of Stratford upon Avon.

However, there are elements that seem more Mediterranean than British. The theme of 'honour' running through the play seems to suit the setting, both in the sense of Hero's virginity and in the sense of the importance of reputation.

The play is set at the end of a war. Modern productions have set it in all sorts of periods, from Elizabethan to the Second World War. The sense that the war is over and that it is time for rest and romance is very important in establishing the atmosphere of the play. It is set mainly outside in the gardens of Leonato's house and the mood at the start is sunny and playful.

Shakespeare: Settings

However, there is a snake in the garden, as in the Garden of Eden, in the form of Don John. His plotting reminds us that it is not always easy to forgive and forget. It is a footnote to the war in which he has been defeated by his brother, Don Pedro.

Just as the garden and the masked ball have symbolic meanings, so does the chapel where Hero and Claudio are to be married. The sacred setting makes Claudio's deed even worse. When the same setting is used for his penance and for their reconciliation, these events are also made holy.

Macbeth

Macbeth is based on accounts of the life of a real man, who was King of Scotland from 1040 to 1057. By the time the story reached Shakespeare it was difficult to tell fact from fiction, but it is true that Macbeth did kill Duncan. It is less certain whether Banquo existed, but he is an important part of the play because he was said to be the ancestor of King James VI of Scotland, who succeeded Queen Elizabeth I in 1603 as King James I of England. Shakespeare wrote *Macbeth* not long after this succession.

James I was the patron of Shakespeare's theatre company and it was obviously a good idea to please him. So *Macbeth* includes two themes which were very dear to James's heart: witches and the divine right of kings. Like many people at the time, James firmly believed in witches and had even written a book about them. He also believed in the divine right of kings, meaning that he thought his authority came from God. Because of this, the murder of a king would be considered a very serious sin.

By upsetting the proper order of things, Macbeth creates chaos in his country. James might well have hoped that people who were challenging his authority would have taken note.

Scotland is seen as a harsh place with its great castles and its 'blasted heath', so is a suitable setting for violence, murder and witchcraft. The wild weather, controlled by the witches, reflects the chaos that comes to the kingdom with the murder of Duncan.

Shakespeare: Settings

Twelfth Night

Twelfth Night is another name for the feast of the Epiphany, celebrated on 6th January, which traditionally marked the end of the Christmas season. It was a time for eating, drinking, playing games and practical jokes. Christmas is not mentioned in the play, but the spirit of the season is present in the disguises, confusion and the cruel trick played on Malvolio. There is also a sense of time and the seasons passing.

Illyria, where the play is set, is a Roman name for an area roughly where Albania, Croatia and Serbia are today. In the play it is a strange, even dream-like place, where people act oddly. The audience experiences it with Viola, who has been washed up on the coast, having lost her brother. There are two courts – of Olivia and Orsino – where life seems almost to stand still as Orsino poses as an unrequited lover and Olivia mourns her dead brother.

Olivia's household is unruly. The servants are in charge and the guests have overstayed their welcome. While the higher status characters belong to a sort of fairy tale world, the comic characters are versions of the sort of 'hangers on' that Shakespeare might have met in the country houses and palaces of England. Social status is very important to everyone, from Orsino down to Maria and Feste, but none of them behaves quite in the way that Elizabethan society would expect.

Key scenes take place in a garden (as they often do in Shakespeare's comedies). Olivia's garden is the scene of Olivia's meeting with the disguised Viola, the trick played on Malvolio, and Olivia's meeting with Sebastian.

Julius Caesar

Shakespeare set several plays in ancient Rome. His main source was the work of Plutarch, who wrote not long after Caesar's death, so his version of history is quite accurate. Shakespeare wrote many plays about power and authority and the ideas discussed in them are just as relevant now as they were then. When the play was first performed, towards the end of the reign of Elizabeth I, there had been several attempts to get rid of the Queen. Historical plays were a forum for discussing ideas and issues that it might not be wise to discuss openly.

In some ways, though, ancient Rome was very different from Elizabethan England. The Roman Republic, which is put in danger by Caesar's increasing power, was not what we would call a democracy – slaves and women had no say in politics – but it was probably more democratic than the England of Shakespeare's day. Its complex political system is portrayed quite accurately: the roles of senators, tribunes and citizens are all shown. Educated members of Shakespeare's audience would have been familiar with Roman history.

The settings for individual scenes include the streets of Rome, the Capitol (where the senate meets and Caesar is murdered), the Forum (where citizens meet) and the battlefield of Philippi. These are real places where the historical events took place. For each one Shakespeare creates an atmosphere which reflects its role in Roman history. He also sets quieter scenes in the homes of Brutus and Caesar, showing them at home with their wives to give us a sense of them as ordinary men, not just historical figures.

Shakespeare: Genre

Shakespeare wrote over thirty plays covering a range of subjects, set in many different times and places, and in a variety of genres. The plays are often divided into tragedies, comedies and histories, though sometimes these genres overlap.

- *Much Ado About Nothing* and *Twelfth Night* are comedies.
- *Romeo and Juliet, Macbeth* and *Julius Caesar* are tragedies.

You may have come across other plays by Shakespeare. If you have, it is useful to look at a group of plays and think about what they have in common.

- Other examples of tragedies are *Hamlet*, *Othello* and *King Lear.*
- Other comedies are *A Midsummer Night's Dream, As You Like It* and *The Taming of the Shrew.*
- Histories include *Richard II, Henry V* and *Richard III.*

Each genre has its own **conventions.** A convention is not a rule, but it is the way in which things are usually done.

Some elements that often appear in Shakespearean **comedies** are listed below:

- Women dressed as men
- Masks and disguises
- Falling in love with the wrong person
- Families split up or in conflict
- Comic sub-plots, often involving low status characters
- Songs and dances
- Forests or gardens
- People who are thought to be dead coming alive
- Practical jokes
- Fights that could end in tragedy
- An outsider
- Couples getting married at the end

And here are some common elements in Shakespeare's **tragedies:**

- Murder
- Challenges to authority
- The tragic hero
- The fatal flaw (a part of the hero's personality that causes his downfall)
- Premonitions / magic / spells
- Deceit and betrayal
- Chaos in nature
- Families turning against each other
- Fights with tragic consequences
- Some broad comedy
- The main character dying
- Order restored at the end

Which elements do you think are present in your play?

A brief look at these lists will show you that there are some very similar elements in both tragedies and comedies. For example:

- There are masked balls in both *Much Ado About Nothing* and *Romeo and Juliet.*
- There are fights in both *Twelfth Night* and *Romeo and Juliet.*
- The king is overthrown in *Macbeth,* and Don John in *Much Ado About Nothing* has tried to take his brother's place as Prince.

The difference between comedy and tragedy lies in the outcome of these things. In comedies, misunderstandings are straightened out, people learn the errors of their ways, everyone gets married and the play ends with the promise of a happier future. In tragedies, the misunderstandings lead to death, and people repent only with their last breath. Most of them die at the end, although the play still ends with the promise of a better future.

Shakespeare: Form

Structure

Most of Shakespeare's plots follow a similar pattern, whether they are comedies or tragedies.

1 The scene is set and the main characters introduced.

2 Something happens that really starts the story and will change the characters' lives (especially the protagonist's):
- In *Macbeth* the witches tell Macbeth that he will become King of Scotland.
- In *Twelfth Night* Viola is sent by Orsino to woo Olivia, but Viola realises that she in fact loves Orsino.

3 Something happens to complicate the plot, usually making things difficult for the protagonist:
- In *Romeo and Juliet* Romeo kills Tybalt.
- Mark Antony gets the support of the citizens in *Julius Caesar*.

4 Things get more and more complicated but the characters try to sort it out:
- In *Much Ado About Nothing* Beatrice tells Benedick to kill Claudio.
- In *Romeo and Juliet* Juliet drinks Friar Lawrence's potion.

5 The play reaches a climax where everything comes to a conclusion whether happily or unhappily:
- In *Twelfth Night* Viola meets Sebastian, reveals that she is a girl and marries Orsino.
- In *Macbeth* Macduff kills Macbeth and Malcolm becomes king of Scotland.

You will have noticed that there are five points, one for each act of the play. Shakespeare's five act structure does usually work along these lines, with each act generally ending on a turning point in the plot.

Some plays, mainly the comedies, have a number of lesser plots that run parallel to and complement the main plot, for example Sir Toby and Maria's revenge on Malvolio in *Twelfth Night*.

Beginnings

Look at the first act and think about the opening of the play and how Shakespeare sets the scene and introduces the characters:
- When and how do we find out where the play is set?
- What mood or atmosphere is created in the opening scenes? How?
- What do we learn about the main characters in the opening scenes?
- How does Shakespeare build up tension and anticipation?

Putting a Scene in Context

If you are focusing on a particular scene, think about where it fits into the plot:
- What has happened already and how has the situation in this scene come about?
- What happens in the scene to change things? Is this an important turning point in the plot?
- What happens afterwards and how is the unfolding plot influenced by this scene?

Endings

When you look at the end of the play you might consider the following:
- How this ending has come about
- What happens to each of the main characters and why
- How the ending makes you feel and whether it is a satisfactory conclusion to the play.

Preparation Task

To help you to remember the plot accurately, do a summary in the form of a comic strip or storyboard. You could have one frame for each scene or limit yourself to a smaller number. You could also find a quotation for each frame and illustrate it.

Shakespeare: Language

Whether your question focuses on a character from the play or a theme, you will be expected to comment on Shakespeare's use of language. This will show that you understand how Shakespeare conveys thoughts, feelings and ideas.

Prose and Verse

Shakespeare wrote in a mixture of prose and verse. It should be obvious which is being used in a passage simply by the look of it. Verse has definite line endings and a regular **rhythm**. Sometimes it **rhymes.**

Most of the verse in Shakespeare is written in **iambic pentameter**. That means there are five stressed beats to each line, the stress being on every second syllable. If you read a few lines aloud the beats should naturally fall into this pattern:

> I cannot tell what you and other men
> Think of this life; but for my single self
> I had as lief not be as live to be
> In awe of such a thing as I myself
> *(Julius Caesar* Act 1 scene 2)

The iambic pentameter is perhaps the metre that follows most closely the natural rhythms of speech. It is often said to resemble a heartbeat. You will sometimes find variations on this strict metre – for example the first syllable in a line being stressed or an extra syllable added at the end of the line. Think about what effect this has.

Rhyme is used to end a scene or emphasise the importance of a pair of lines:

> O time, thou must untangle this, not I:
> It is too hard a knot for me t'untie.
> *(Twelfth Night* Act 2 scene 2)

Generally speaking, verse is spoken by high status characters when they discuss serious issues. Prose is spoken by lower status characters and by high status characters when they are joking.

When Shakespeare uses forms other than the iambic pentameter it is for songs, for example by Feste in *Twelfth Night* or the witches in *Macbeth*.

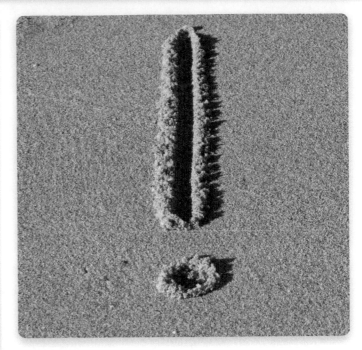

Punctuation

Sometimes there will be a **pause** in the middle of a line, perhaps marked by a **full stop** or comma to indicate a change of subject or mood. **Dashes, colons** and **semi colons** can break up the speech, making it hesitant or jerky. Banquo's speech before the murder of Duncan reflects his concern that something is wrong:

> Hold, take my sword - There's husbandry in heaven:
> Their candles are all out: - take thee that too.
> *(Macbeth* Act 2 scene 1)

Sounds

Listen to the sound of Shakespeare's words and think about the mood created and how it is achieved. The rhythm of the verse helps to create the sound, as does rhyme. Shakespeare also uses alliteration to create a certain tone:

> Will I with wine and wassail so convince
> That memory, the warder of the brain
> *(Macbeth* Act 1 scene 7)

The 'w' and 'v' sounds here slide into each other and give a sense of the sleepy drunkenness of the men guarding Duncan.

Shakespeare: Language

Diction and Imagery

The characters' diction (or choice of words) can tell us a lot about how they are feeling. In Shakespeare they tend to use a lot of imagery.

Imagery
Look for patterns in the imagery which might tell you something about the speaker and the general mood of the scene.

For example, Claudio uses a **simile** that compares Hero to both the Roman goddess of love and to animals. This expresses his lack of respect for her and is shocking to the audience, which knows she is innocent:

> But you are more intemperate in your blood
> Than Venus or those pamper'd animals
> That rage in savage sensuality
>   (*Much Ado About Nothing* Act 4 scene 1)

Romeo, in contrast, expresses his love for Juliet by using metaphors that make his love seem holy, like that of a pilgrim for a saint:

> If I profane with my unworthiest hand
> This holy shrine…
>   (*Romeo and Juliet* Act 1 scene 5)

Rhetorical Language

Rhetorical questions (questions which do not require an answer) are often used when characters are thinking about something – perhaps asking themselves what they should do: 'I have railed so long against marriage; but doth not the appetite alter?' (*Much Ado About Nothing* Act 2 scene 2)

Repetition is often used to good effect to draw attention to an important idea or feeling: 'Tomorrow, and tomorrow and tomorrow'. (*Macbeth* Act 5 scene 5)

When a character is trying to change someone's mind or sway an audience, he/she might use the **rule of three**: 'Friends, Romans, countrymen, lend me your ears'. (Julius *Caesar* Act 3 scene 2)

Techniques like these are used a lot in *Julius Caesar*, reflecting the fact that the main characters are politicians who use rhetoric (the art of speech) to put across their points of view.

Playing with Language
The example bottom left shows Romeo 'playing with' language. Romeo and Juliet develop the metaphor of the pilgrim, making it more and more complicated. This is sometimes referred to as a **conceit**. Many characters in Shakespeare test their wit against each other by trying to be clever with language.

Oxymorons (two words with opposite meanings put together for effect) were popular in Shakespeare's time: 'pure impiety and impious purity'. (*Much Ado About Nothing* Act 4 scene 3).

Characters often use **puns** and double meanings to make their points. Benedick and Beatrice in *Much Ado About Nothing* do this a lot, as do Romeo and Mercutio in *Romeo and Juliet*.

Double meanings are also used in a cruder way to make sexual innuendoes. This sort of language is sometimes referred to as **bawdy language.**

A lot of the jokes in Shakespeare are lost on modern audiences because of the change in the meaning of words over the years. Because of this modern actors often rely on gestures to get the meaning across.

Helpful Hint

It is good to use the correct terminology when you write about language, but you must also explain the effect of the techniques you have spotted.

The English Literary Heritage

'Literary Heritage' texts are texts written by writers whose reputations are established. They are not necessarily from England. They could be from Wales, Scotland, Ireland or even America. They are part of the English Literary Heritage because they wrote in English and their work is seen as part of the tradition of English literature.

The authors on the 'approved list' wrote over a wide time period, from Geoffrey Chaucer, who wrote in the fourteenth century, to writers who were still writing at the beginning of the twenty first century. Many things have changed over the past seven hundred years, not least the English language itself. So you may, if you are studying one of the older texts, find some of the language unfamiliar.

You may also find the way in which the characters live and act very different from the way people live now. Whichever unit you are taking, it is important that you focus on the society in which the text is set.

In this section of the guide we will look at the following aspects of study:
- Settings
- Ideas, themes and issues
- Character
- Genre and form
- Language and technique

Each aspect will be considered in the light of the texts' social context.

If you are studying Unit 3 (**The Significance of Shakespeare and the English Literary Heritage**) you can study any text from an author listed on page 95, as long as you have not studied it for any other unit of the course. It could be a novel, a collection of short stories, a play or a collection of poetry.

If you are taking Unit 4 (**Approaching Shakespeare and the English Literary Heritage**) you will have studied one of the following texts:
- *Pride and Prejudice* by Jane Austen (1775–1817)
- *Wuthering Heights* by Emily Brontë (1818–1848)
- *Great Expectations* by Charles Dickens (1812–1870)
- *The Withered Arm and Other Wessex Tales* by Thomas Hardy (1840–1928)
- *Animal Farm* by George Orwell (1903–1950)

All of these writers were greatly influenced by their backgrounds and the sort of society they lived in. They wrote about the people and places they knew. Their work reflects the ideas and issues that were current when they wrote. They were influenced by writers who went before them and by the artistic and literary fashions of their times. They, in turn, influenced and inspired other writers.

If you have not done so already, it is well worth doing some research on the life and times of your chosen author.

All the examples used in the following pages are taken from the five texts that have been set for the exam.

The ELH: Ideas, Themes and Issues

When you re-read your text, think about how the attitudes and ideas expressed in it differ from those you might expect today. Below are some areas you might look at. What other ideas, themes and issues are explored in your text?

Men and Women

- In *Pride and Prejudice* the women sew, draw, read, go for walks and dance. The men, in contrast are very active. Rich Mr Darcy runs his estates, while Wickham and Mr Collins have 'professions': the Army and the Church respectively. However, in social relations things are much more equal. Intellectually, Elizabeth is Darcy's equal and he admires her for it.

- In *Wuthering Heights* Cathy's behaviour is certainly not what would be expected of a woman of her class. We also see examples of working class women, like Nelly. Among the men we have the extremes of the brutal Heathcliff and the weak Linton. One might be said to be too masculine while the other is not masculine enough.

- In *Great Expectations* Miss Havisham is an example of a woman who has declared war on men. She has been soured by experience and wants revenge. Pip sees many different examples of how men behave while he himself is learning to be a man.

- Thomas Hardy's women are usually the sympathetic characters. They are often the victims of men or just of their own lack of power. Both the women in *The Withered Arm* are victims, as is Phyllis in *The Melancholy Hussar of The German Legion*. On the other hand, Lizzy in *The Distracted Preacher* is independent and spirited.

- Although most of the characters in *Animal Farm* are not human, they can be seen to be taking traditional male and female roles. Female characters, such as Clover, Mollie and Muriel, do not take a major part in the action. Similarly, women have not usually taken a major role in revolutions and governments until quite recently.

The Family and Children

- In *Pride and Prejudice* Elizabeth is devoted to Jane and her father, but at times embarrassed by the rest of her family.

  Other families also influence the plot. Mr Bingley's sisters try to put him off Jane, while Lady Catherine regards it as her duty to stop Elizabeth marrying into her family.

- In *Wuthering Heights* the Earnshaws are a happy family at first, but everything is changed by the arrival of Heathcliff. In contrast to the Earnshaws, the Lintons are wealthy and well-mannered but very weak. Heathcliff's childhood turns him into a monster and he almost destroys two families.

- The families in *Great Expectations* are not conventional. Pip is an orphan living with his sister, while Estella does not know that her father is alive. Childhood is full of dangers in Dickens, as it was for most children at the time. Those in charge of children can be mentally and physically cruel, but they can also be kind like Joe Gargery.

- Families in Thomas Hardy's stories often consist of one parent and one child: Rhoda and her son in *The Withered Arm*, for example, or Sophy and her son in *The Son's Veto*. These relationships are close but not always happy.

- There are no 'families' in *Animal Farm*, although the characters tend to identify with other animals of the same breed. Early in the book, Jessie and Bluebell's puppies are taken from them to be indoctrinated by the pigs, perhaps reflecting a disregard for family life in communist countries.

Class and Money

- The Bennet sisters have to marry for financial reasons. Everybody in *Pride and Prejudice* knows how much money everybody else has. Everybody also knows where he / she stands in terms of class. Lady Catherine de Burgh is at the top and the Bennets a long way below.

- The Earnshaws in *Wuthering Heights* are from a class that was disappearing in the early nineteenth century. They are farmers and they treat their servants almost as family, but they are also seen as equals by the wealthy Lintons. Heathcliff, with his mysterious origins, is completely outside the class system. In the end he is the wealthiest and most powerful character.

- In *Great Expectations* Pip comes from a poor family but wants to be a gentleman. When he comes into his fortune he finds that money is not everything and that people's worth should not be judged by their class.

- Hardy's sympathies lie with the rural poor. He shows not only the harshness of their life, but also their cleverness and spirit, as seen in *Tony Kytes, the Arch-Deceiver* and *The Distracted Preacher*.

- Class issues are central to *Animal Farm*. The animals unite against the ruling class of the humans, who are the equivalent of the aristocrats of early twentieth century Russia and Europe. However, power corrupts the pigs, who started the revolution, and they become like the humans. Characters like Boxer, who represent the working classes, are now looked down on by the animals who were supposed to support them. Money is also important. Instead of running the farm for the benefit of all animals, the pigs become greedy, seeking to make money for themselves just as the farmer did.

Love and Marriage

- In *Pride and Prejudice* Mrs Bennet wants to get all her daughters married. Austen shows two marriages which could have been Elizabeth's. Her friend Charlotte Lucas does not love Mr Collins but she sees him as her best chance of a settled future. Lydia, on the other hand, scandalously elopes with Wickham with no thought for security. The marriage of Elizabeth and Darcy is a love match, but also a very sensible one.

- In *Wuthering Heights* Cathy and Heathcliff's love is dangerous and destructive. They both marry people they do not love and who become their victims. It takes another generation before anyone is happily married, but Cathy and Heathcliff's love lives on after them.

- In *Great Expectations* Pip's love for Estella does not make him happy and, although she comes to realise his worth, we cannot be sure they will have a 'happy ending'. Miss Havisham's experience has left her bitter and Joe's wife gives him a hard time. However, at least Joe eventually finds happiness with Biddy.

- In Hardy marriage is rarely a happy ending. Sophy in *The Son's Veto* marries a man from a higher class and becomes trapped. In *The Withered Arm* Gertrude Lodge's growing unhappiness is symbolised by the state of her arm.

Helpful Hint

When you write about ideas and attitudes in the past, make sure that everything you say is rooted in the text itself, perhaps supported by known facts from your research.

The ELH: Characters

Questions in both the examination and the controlled assessment often ask you to write about characters. You will need to consider the following:

- What they are like
- What they do
- How they fit into society
- Their function in the text

All the set texts feature a wide range of characters. You could be asked about the main characters, such as Elizabeth Bennet from *Pride and Prejudice* or Tony Kytes in *Tony Kytes, the Arch-Deceiver.* You might be asked to write about less important characters, possibly more than one of them, such as Magwitch in *Great Expectations* or Nelly Dean and Joseph in *Wuthering Heights.*

Characters in Society

Whichever text you are studying, you should make sure you understand how a character fits into the society depicted in the text. You could ask the following questions:

- What is his / her status in society? In *Pride and Prejudice* Darcy, because of his money and land, has a very high status. Joseph in *Wuthering Heights* is a servant and therefore has low status.
- What difference does the character's gender make? Sophy in *The Son's Veto* is dependent on men and limited by being female, as are most of the women in these texts. Lady Catherine de Burgh in *Pride and Prejudice,* however, is powerful in spite of her sex; her wealth is more important.
- Is he / she comfortable in their society? Nearly all Jane Austen's characters seem at first to be at ease in their world, but are they really? Both Cathy in *Wuthering Heights* and Estella in *Great Expectations* defy the expectations for women of their class.
- Is the character outside society? Rhoda Brook in *The Withered Arm*, Magwitch in *Great Expectations* and Heathcliff in *Wuthering Heights* are all outsiders whose actions have far-reaching effects for others.

Characters in Novels

In both *Pride and Prejudice* and *Great Expectations* the main characters change a good deal. They learn about themselves and the world they live in. The main characters in *Wuthering Heights* also learn from their mistakes but they learn too late and their lives end in tragedy.

As you read a longer text is a good idea to keep 'character logs' for all the main characters (see page 20). By looking back at these you will see how these characters are presented and how they have changed during the course of the novel. You should also have some useful references to the text, supporting your points.

When you look at minor characters, think about why they are in the novel. Do they do something significant which influences the plot? How do they relate to the main characters? What do they represent?

As a revision exercise, it can be helpful to list all the less important characters in the novel and make a chart like the one opposite, which has been partly completed.

Characters in Short Stories

In short stories there are not as many characters as in novels, nor are they developed in as much depth. However, you will still find that some characters change due to their experiences, for example, Mrs Lodge in *The Withered Arm* or Stockdale in *The Distracted Preacher.* Others do not change much, but we get to know a little more about them and how others see them.

In the exam the questions on short stories will always be about more than one story. When you choose your second story, think about which one contains a character or characters that you can confidently compare to those in the named story.

Think about which characters you can link and how they can be linked. Below is a list of possible links between characters in *The Withered Arm and Other Wessex Tales*:

- **Mothers**: Rhoda Brook (*The Withered Arm*), Sophy Twycott (*The Son's Veto*), Mrs Simpkins (*The Distracted Preacher*)
- **Fathers**: Lodge (*The Withered Arm*), Mr Twycott (*The Son's Veto*), Old Mr Kytes (*Tony Kytes, the Arch-Deceiver*), Dr Grove (*The Melancholy Hussar of the German Legion*)
- **Sons:** Rhoda's son (*The Withered Arm*), Randolph Twycott (*The Son's Veto*), Tony Kytes (*Tony Kytes, the Arch-Deceiver*)
- **People from outside Wessex:** Mr Twycott (*The Son's Veto*), Matthaus Tina and Humphrey Gould (*The Melancholy Hussar of the German Legion*), Stockdale (*The Distracted Preacher*)

The ELH: Characters

- **Women in love:**
- **Men in love:**
- **Comic characters:**
- **Tragic characters:**

If you are studying *The Withered Arm and Other Wessex Tales* think about which characters from the tales fit the last four categories. Are there any other links you could make?

Character Chart for *Pride and Prejudice*

Character	What he / she is like	What he / she does	Place in Society	Function
Jane Bennet	Reliable, loyal, shy, kind-hearted	Falls in love with Bingley and is rejected at first.		Elizabeth's confidante; she forms a contrast with Elizabeth; her romance runs parallel to Elizabeth's.
Bingley	Honest, generous, loyal, but too easily influenced.		He is the richest man in the neighbourhood and the centre of social life; his family has not been rich for long.	
Lydia Bennet	Silly and reckless	Runs away with Wickham		Her actions affect the whole family; Darcy shows his love for Elizabeth by finding Lydia and making Wickham marry her.
Wickham	Charming, dishonest, poor	Flirts with everybody; deceives people; seduces Lydia		
Mr Collins	Snobbish, boring, serious		As a clergyman he is respectable, but not rich. He is dependent on Lady Catherine.	
Charlotte Lucas	Pleasant but plain; realistic	Makes a sensible marriage to Mr Collins		
Mr Bennet		Very little!		If he dies the girls will have nothing, so they must find good husbands.
Mrs Bennet	Ambitious, chatty, domineering			
Lady Catherine de Burgh			The character that is highest in the social order.	

The ELH: Settings

It is important when reading your text from the English Literary Heritage that you pay attention not only to when it is set but also where it is set. Think about the effect the setting has on the characters and plot, and how it creates mood and atmosphere.

Many novels and stories are set in the places where the writers lived and worked. If you get a chance, it is useful and interesting to visit the 'real' setting.

Pride and Prejudice

Pride and Prejudice is set in Hertfordshire. Austen is only really concerned with the middle classes and their lives seem to be quiet, contented and a bit dull. Everybody seems to know everybody else, so when Mr Bingley rents the biggest house in the area, there is great excitement.

There are two important balls in the novel: an informal one at Meryton and a grander one at Netherfield, Bingley's house. These balls provide Austen with a formal setting where she can explore the manners and behaviour of her characters.

The various houses in *Pride and Prejudice* tell us much about their inhabitants, especially their social status. The Bennets' house at Longbourn is seen as comfortable but comparatively small. Netherfield is much more impressive, but is not nearly as grand as Rosings, Lady Catherine de Burgh's house.

One of the key episodes of the novel is Elizabeth's trip to Pemberley, the home of Mr Darcy. The trip to Derbyshire with her aunt and uncle reflects a new fashion for visiting the countryside. The house and grounds seem to convince Elizabeth that she is in love with Darcy. Is it because they give her a glimpse of the 'real' Darcy?

Wuthering Heights

The fact that the novel takes its name from a place shows how important setting is in *Wuthering Heights*.

Wuthering Heights is described as remote, wild and far from civilisation. When the novel opens Heathcliff is the owner of the house and the descriptions reflect the atmosphere of cruelty and mystery that surrounds him. Yet, according to Nelly Dean, it used to be a happy family home.

Thrushcross Grange provides a contrast with Wuthering Heights. It is set in a park, protected and cultivated, rather than high on the moors.

For the young Cathy it represents everything that her home does not. However, when she moves there as Edgar Linton's wife, she is unhappy and she longs for the freedom of the moors around Wuthering Heights.

The landscape is beautiful and terrifying. The descriptions of the moors and the wild weather reflect the strong emotions of Cathy and Heathcliff.

Yet, at the very end there is a sense of peace and continuity, as Lockwood wonders 'how anyone could ever imagine unquiet slumbers for the sleepers in that quiet earth'.

The Withered Arm and Other Wessex Tales

Wessex is the name Hardy gave to the area of South West England where he lived for most of his life. Most of the places in his tales are fictional but are based on real places, mostly in Dorset. Hardy describes the rugged countryside of the heath, but also the farms and villages of the area.

When the setting is outside Wessex (as in *The Son's Veto*) the characters tend to come from Wessex and long to return.

At the time that Hardy wrote, Dorset was a rural county with most people dependent on the land for a living. The Wessex tales include the whole of Wessex society, from squires and vicars, through farmers and milkmaids to smugglers and even the hangman.

Life is harsh for many people and it is the poor and those who do not fit in that Hardy has sympathy for. The rigid class system of the time causes injustice and unhappiness.

However, he also shows the positive, light-hearted side of village life in stories such as *Absent-mindedness in a Parish Choir* and *The Distracted Preacher.*

Animal Farm

The setting of *Animal Farm* is a typical farm in England in the early twentieth century. However, the farm could be said to be a **microcosm** of any society or nation, especially Russia before and after the revolution of 1917.

Different locations on the farm are important. The fact that the pigs move into the farmhouse shows that they see themselves as the rulers of the farm even before they begin to act like humans. The barn is where meetings take place and at first might seem to represent freedom and democracy, but later slogans are painted on its walls and it becomes part of the pigs' oppression of the other animals.

Towards the end of the story we become more aware of the world outside Animal Farm. The neighbouring farms start to have an influence on what is going on in Animal Farm, just as Britain, America and Germany had an impact on the Soviet Union.

Great Expectations

Great Expectations opens with a frightening scene in a graveyard when Magwitch appears out of the gloom. This sets the tone for the first part of the novel, which is set in 'the marsh country' of Kent. This is a bleak, grey landscape, which reflects the lack of affection in Pip's childhood and symbolises the dangers that the world holds for him. The warm and welcoming blacksmith's forge forms a contrast with this.

The houses described in *Great Expectations* reflect the personalities of those who live there. Miss Havisham's house is dark, empty and unchanged in years. In contrast, the Pockets' home is pleasant, untidy and full of children.

There is contrast too between Pip's life in Kent and the new life he finds in London. Nineteenth century London, with its huge population, extremes of wealth and poverty, and its opportunities and dangers, is seen through Pip's eyes as he starts his journey through life. As he discovers London, he discovers himself and what matters to him, before returning home to the marshes.

The ELH: Genre and Form

Genre

Today when we talk about genre, we are usually referring to a particular kind of text, written for a particular audience, for example science fiction or teenage romance. If we know what genre a text belongs to, we know what to expect. Each genre has its own traditions and conventions.

The text you have been studying for this unit may not fit quite so easily into a genre, but all the writers in the English Literary Heritage were influenced by the ideas and fashions of their time, just as writers are today.

How would you describe your text in terms of genre?

- *Pride and Prejudice* is often thought of as a **romance.** Two people meet; they love each other but don't know it; they overcome obstacles; and they get married in the end. However, it is also very funny and can be seen as **satire**, because Austen uses humour to criticise people and society.

- *Wuthering Heights*, too, is a romance, but a different sort of romance. Cathy and Heathcliff's love affair is **tragic**, not comic. There are many elements of the gothic tradition, which had been popular in the early nineteenth century. Lonely settings, ghosts, violence and dark, mysterious heroes are all elements of the **gothic**.

- You might also see a gothic influence in *Great Expectations*, especially in the scenes with Magwitch and Miss Havisham, as well as some elements of **romance**, **comedy** and **adventure**. However, the novel is primarily about Pip's experience of life and what he learns. Novels like this – popular in the Victorian period – are sometimes called by the German word **bildungsroman.**

- Hardy draws on many traditions. Some of his stories are amusing **anecdotes**, possibly based on real stories that had been passed on to him. Other tales are **tragic romances**, drawing on traditional stories and the gothic tradition.

- Orwell called *Animal Farm* a **fable**, which is a story that conveys a moral message. Aesop's Fables also used animal characters. *Animal Farm* is often seen as an 'allegory' of the history of the Russian Revolution.

Structure

Look again at the discussion of story structure on page 27. Try to write a summary or make a storyboard of the main plot of your text. If you are studying short stories, it is quite easy to pick out the main events of each plot. If you have studied a novel, you may find that there are quite a few turning points. You may also identify 'sub plots' running alongside the main plot.

Most of the texts in this section follow a straightforward chronological structure. They start at the beginning of the story and tell it in order. *Wuthering Heights*, however, starts towards the end of the story, with Lockwood visiting Wuthering Heights before he hears the story of Cathy and Heathcliff from Nelly. *The Withered Arm* also starts part way through the story before going back to the beginning.

Think about why a writer might structure his/her text in an unusual way and the effect it has on your reading of the text.

The ELH: Language and Techniques

Narrative Style

What sort of narrator does your text have?

- *Pride and Prejudice* is written in the third person. Jane Austen is an **omniscient**, or all-knowing narrator and can tell us anyone's thoughts. However, she sometimes chooses not to. She also, once or twice, speaks directly to the reader.
- *Great Expectations* is a **first person narrative,** with the narrator being the main character. We only know what he knows.
- *Wuthering Heights* is written in the first person, but has several narrators. Lockwood, who starts the story, has little or nothing to do with it. He is told most of the story by Nelly Dean. Some parts of the story are told to Nelly by other characters.
- Thomas Hardy varies his narrative style from story to story. If you are studying his short stories, it is a good idea to make a list of which are first and which are third person narratives.

Think about why the writer uses a particular narrative style. What difference does it make to your experience of the novel if…

- a character is telling his / her own story?
- there are several narrators?
- you know the thoughts and feelings of more than one character?
- you are aware of the character and the attitudes of the narrator?

Language

When you consider the language used in your text, it might be useful to think about the following points.

The language used by the narrator

What kind of tone does the narrator use?

- Friendly
- Colloquial
- Formal
- Ironic

As you are reading the text, do you feel that the narrator is speaking to you personally?

Speech

Does the way in which the characters speak make a difference to your understanding of them and to the general tone of the novel?

Do any of them do the following?

- Use dialect words and phrases.
- Use language in a deliberately comic way.
- Have oddities or peculiarities of speech.
- Use 'catch phrases'.
- Use over-formal language.
- Use language which others might not understand.

Some writers use a lot of dialogue, others very little. Think about when and why direct speech might be used.

Descriptive Language

When you read descriptive passages in your text, you should consider how the writer uses techniques similar to those used by poets to create mood and atmosphere. You might find the following:

- A mixture of short and long sentences
- Telling use of detail
- Alliteration and assonance
- Imagery
- Symbolism

These techniques are used to describe people as well as places.

Preparation Task

Choose a short passage which describes a place and analyse how the writer uses language to create a mood or atmosphere.

Then find a description of a person and analyse how the writer uses language to convey his / her character.

Exam Tips

The exam is called **Unit 4: Approaching Shakespeare and the English Literary Heritage.**

It is in two sections: **Section A** is on Shakespeare and **Section B** is on Prose from the English Literary Heritage.
- You cannot take your texts into the examination hall.
- You will not be allowed to take any other texts or additional notes in with you.

Before the exam make sure that you:
- Know both your Shakespeare play and your prose text well. You should read each one two or three times before the exam.
- Have read the notes you have taken or been given in class and that you understand them.
- Have come up with your own ideas about the texts – the examiner wants to know what you think, not what your teacher thinks.
- Have identified and put right errors that you know you make in punctuation, grammar and spelling.
- Have completed the essential preparation and essential practice tasks given in this section of the guide.
- Have perfected the PEE technique.
- Are able to write confidently about ideas, themes and issues; characters; form and structure; language and technique.

Section A

In the exam, make sure that you:
- Are aware of the time: you should spend **45 minutes** on Section A. It is helpful to spend a few minutes planning what you are going to write.
- Quickly find the questions on the play you have studied.
- Read the two questions on your play carefully. Choose one that you fully understand and you feel you can answer well.
- Only answer questions on the play you have studied.
- Annotate the text reproduced on the question paper by underlining, highlighting and/or making brief notes.
- Write in paragraphs.
- Refer closely to the text, using PEE.
- Check your work carefully for errors.

If you are doing **Foundation Tier**:
- Remember that your question is in two parts – effectively two short essays. Answer both parts.
- Divide your time equally between the two parts (just over 20 minutes for each).
- Make sure that both parts of your answer focus on the extract.

If you are doing **Higher Tier:**
- In Section A there are two parts to the question. Answer both parts.
- Divide your time equally between the two parts (roughly 20 minutes each).
- Make sure that your answer to part (a) focuses on the extract.
- Choose the section to write about for part (b) carefully. Choose a scene or passage you know well, making sure that it fits the question.

For guidance on key words and phrases used in exams see page 29.

Answer one of the questions below in 45 minutes, choosing either the Foundation Tier or the Higher Tier question on the extract below it. If neither of the questions is about your text, try finding a short passage from your play and making up your own question.

On the following two pages you will find…
- a writing frame for part (a) of one of these questions, which will help you to understand how a good answer is organised
- an answer to part (b) of another question.

Question 1 (Foundation Tier)

Answer both parts (a) and (b)

Part (a) How does Shakespeare show you Lady Macbeth's thoughts and feelings in the passage below? In your answer you should write about:
- What Lady Macbeth's thoughts and feelings are.
- How Shakespeare shows these thoughts and feelings through the way he writes.

Part (b) Write about Lady Macbeth's thoughts and feelings in another part of the play.

Question 1 (Higher Tier)

Answer both parts (a) and (b)

Part (a) How does Shakespeare show Lady Macbeth's thoughts and feelings in the passage below?

Part (b) How does Shakespeare show Lady Macbeth in a different way at another point in the play?

> LADY MACBETH:
>
>   The raven himself is hoarse
> That croaks the fatal entrance of Duncan
> Under my battlements. Come, you spirits
> That tend on mortal thoughts, unsex me here;
> And fill me, from the crown to the toe, top-fill
> Of direst cruelty! Make thick my blood,
> Stop up the access and passage to remorse,
> That no contemptuous visitings of nature
> Shake my fell purpose, nor keep peace between
> The effect and it! Come to my woman's breasts,
> And take my milk for gall, you murdering ministers,
> Wherever your sightless substances
> You wait on nature's mischief! Come, thick night,
> And pall thee in the dunnest smoke of hell,
> That my keen knife sees not the wound it makes,
> Nor heaven peep through the blanket of the dark,
> To cry, Hold, hold!

Question 2 (Foundation Tier)

Answer both parts (a) and (b)

Part (a) How does Shakespeare show us the relationship between Romeo and Juliet in the passage below? You should write about:
- Romeo and Juliet's relationship at this stage in the play.
- How Shakespeare shows this relationship through the way he writes.

Part (b) Write about Romeo and Juliet's relationship in another part of the play.

Question 2 (Higher Tier)

Answer both parts (a) and (b)

Part (a) How does Shakespeare convey Romeo and Juliet's relationship, character and mood in the following extract?

Part (b) Show how Shakespeare presents different aspects of Romeo and Juliet's relationship, character and mood in another part of the play.

> JULIET
> Wilt thou be gone? It is not yet near day.
> It was the nightingale and not the lark
> That pierc'd the fearful hollow of thine ear.
> Nightly she sings on yon pomegranate tree.
> Believe me, love, it was the nightingale.
>
> ROMEO
> It was the lark, the herald of the morn,
> No nightingale: look, love, what envious streaks
> Do lace the severing clouds in yonder east.
> Night's candles are burnt out and jocund day
> Stands tiptoe on the misty mountain tops.
> I must be gone and live, or stay and die.
>
> JULIET
> Yon light is not daylight, I know it, I.
> It is some meteor that the sun exhales,
> To be to thee this night a torch-bearer,
> And light thee on thy way to Mantua,
> Therefore stay yet, thou need'st not be gone.
>
> ROMEO
> Let me be ta'en, let me be put to death.
> I am content, so thou wilt have it so.

Developing Your Answer

Answer both parts (a) and (b)

Part (a) How does Shakespeare show you Lady Macbeth's thoughts and feelings in the passage below?

In your answer you should write about:
- What Lady Macbeth's thoughts and feelings are.
- How Shakespeare shows these thoughts and feelings through the way he writes.

Part (b) Write about Lady Macbeth's thoughts and feelings in another part of the play.

Writing Frame

Writing Frame boxes	Part (a)
Start by explaining what is going on and who she is	Lady Macbeth has just received a letter from her husband, Macbeth, telling her about the witches' prophecies….
Understands what a soliloquy is	Lady Macbeth is alone on stage when she makes this speech. At first she speaks to the audience in a soliloquy…
A clear account of what she is thinking	She has decided that Duncan will be killed when he comes to the castle…
Imagery and symbolism	She uses imagery connected with death. The raven is symbolic of death…
Discusses language using correct terms. Says what the effect is	She talks directly to the 'unseen spirits', using commands. She uses a lot of repetition as she calls on the spirits. She says: 'come' three times. This makes it sound as if she is casting a spell…
Her feelings and thoughts	She wants to be 'unsexed', which means that she does not want to act like a woman would be expected to act…
	She is asking evil spirits to make her evil too so that she does not feel any guilt…
Choice of language and its effect	Her language is very violent and quite shocking. The image of replacing her milk with poison is very strong...
How she feels at the end of the passage	At the end of the speech, she is looking forward to the night so that she can murder Duncan…
	She must know that what she is doing is wrong but she is determined to do it…
Conclusion – the overall impression given by the speech	This is the first time we have seen Lady Macbeth and we are left with an impression of someone who is ruthless and in control, in contrast with Macbeth himself…

This writing frame is designed to give you an idea of the kind of thing you might say and how to organise it. In the exam, you would, of course, expand your points, giving more details and references to the text.

For part **b)** of the question, first choose another scene from the play to write about. Possible scenes include…
- Act 2 scene 1, where Lady Macbeth drugs the guards and urges Macbeth to murder Duncan
- Act 3 scene 1, where Banquo's ghost appears
- Act 5 scene 1, the 'sleepwalking' scene.

Which of these do you think would provide the most interesting comparison with the extract you have been given?

When you have chosen the scene about which you want to write, make a brief plan, perhaps in the form of a writing frame. Then try writing a complete answer to both parts of the question within 40 minutes, remembering to refer closely to the text.

Developing Your Answer

Question 2 (Higher Tier)

Answer both parts (a) and (b)

Part (a) How does Shakespeare convey Romeo and Juliet's relationship, character and mood in the following extract?

Part (b) Show how Shakespeare presents different aspects of Romeo and Juliet's relationship, character and mood in another part of the play.

Part (b)

In this essay I am going to focus on the 'balcony scene'.

At the beginning Romeo is hiding in the orchard. The scene is quiet, in contrast to the ball, and the darkness adds to the atmosphere. When Juliet comes out on to her balcony, it is significant that she is above him because it reflects his feelings about her. He adores her like a goddess. As Juliet cannot hear or see him, Romeo speaks about his love in a soliloquy, so that we know he is telling us his true feelings.

He expresses his feelings by comparing Juliet to the sun, the moon and the stars, for example: 'It is the east and Juliet is the sun'. This imagery shows how great his love is and how natural. He thinks of Juliet as better than anything in nature. He also uses religious images, such as 'angel', as he did when they met. Some people might think this is a bit blasphemous and shows that he loves her too much.

When Juliet speaks, she does not know that Romeo can hear her. She is talking in a soliloquy, so she too is expressing her true feelings. A young lady would not be able to tell a man directly how she felt, so this is a way in which he can find out that she loves him. She wants Romeo to lose his name because she knows that the feud between their families means their love must be secret and dangerous.

When he speaks to her, she is shocked and warns him of the danger he is in, adding to the exciting mood of the scene. However, he says he would rather die than lose her, which foretells the end of the play. So they exchange vows, Juliet using beautiful imagery to express her love:

> My bounty is as boundless as the sea,
> My love as deep...

Like Romeo's imagery the comparison is taken from nature. The use of alliteration and assonance adds emphasis and helps to make the line sound gentle and smooth.

In spite of her strong feelings, Juliet wants proof that he really loves her. Even though she is very young, she is acting in a more mature way than he is by being cautious. They agree to marry then are interrupted by the nurse calling her. This adds to the sense of urgency and danger in the scene.

At the end of the scene we know that Romeo and Juliet are truly in love and that their love is equal. We also know that they will marry in secret and that they have started to move towards their deaths.

Mood

Awareness of the fact that this is a stage play

Their relationship

Correct terms used to make points

Quotations used as part of PEE to support the points that are made

Character

Paragraphs linked effectively

Awareness of historical / social context

Prose from the English Literary Heritage

In the exam, make sure that you:

- Are aware of the time: you should spend **30 minutes** on Section B. It is helpful to spend a few minutes planning what you are going to write.
- Find the question(s) on the prose text you have studied. For the Foundation Tier, there is only one question on each text. For the Higher Tier you will have a choice of two questions.
- Only answer on the text you have studied.
- Write clearly in paragraphs.
- Refer closely to the text.
- Check your work carefully for errors.

If you are doing **Foundation Tier:**

- Remember that your question is in two parts – effectively two short essays. Answer both parts.
- Divide your time equally between the two parts (15 minutes for each).
- Make sure that you write about the society the characters live in.
- If you are writing about short stories, you will be given the title of one story, which you must write about. You then have to write about another story. Choose it carefully, making sure that it fits the question and you can write confidently about it.

If you are doing **Higher Tier:**

- In Section B, there will be a choice of two questions on each set text. You will only answer one question. Choose it carefully.
- Make sure that you write about the society the text is set in.
- If you are writing about short stories, you will be asked to compare two stories. The title of one of them will be given to you. Choose the other carefully, making sure that it fits the question and you can write confidently about it.
- If you are writing about a novel you will sometimes be asked to refer to different parts of the novel. Think carefully about which parts to use, making sure that they are relevant to the question and that you know them well enough to compare them effectively.

Helpful Hints

When referring to the writer always either use his / her surname (Bronte, Dickens, etc.) or refer to him / her as 'the author' or 'the writer'. You can use both first and second names together, but never use the writer's first name alone.

When you mention the title of your text, remember to use capital letters and put it in inverted commas: 'Pride and Prejudice'; 'Great Expectations'; 'The Withered Arm', etc. Notice that little words such as articles (the / a), prepositions (to / at / from, etc.) and conjunctions (and / but, etc.) do not need capitals.

For guidance on key words and phrases used in exams see page 29.

Exam Practice: Section B

For the Section B exam the questions on the Foundation Tier and the Higher Tier are different in style. Make sure that you know which tier you have been entered for.

Answer one of the questions below in 30 minutes, choosing either a Foundation Tier or a Higher Tier question depending on which tier you have been entered for. If none of them is about your text, try making up your own question. When you have finished, ask a teacher or a fellow student to grade your answer.

On the following two pages you will find writing frames for two of these questions.

Foundation Tier Questions

Question 1

Pride and Prejudice

Answer both parts (a) and (b)

Part (a) What impressions do you have of any **two** of the following characters: Lydia Bennet; Mr Bennet; Wickham; Bingley? Remember to write about the society they live in.

Part (b) How does Austen's way of writing create the characters you have chosen?

Question 2

The Withered Arm and Other Wessex Tales

Answer both parts (a) and (b)

Part (a) What impression do you get of the role of women from *The Withered Arm*? Remember to write about the society they live in.

Part (b) How does Hardy's way of writing convey aspects of women's lives in **one** other story?

Question 3

Animal Farm

Answer both parts (a) and (b)

Part (a) What do you find out about the character of Snowball? Remember to write about the society in which he lives.

Part (b) How does Orwell's way of writing create the character of Snowball?

Higher Tier Questions

Question 4

Pride and Prejudice

Referring to **two** different chapters, show how Austen presents social snobbery in the novel.

Remember to write about the society in which the novel is set.

Question 5

Wuthering Heights

How does Brontë convey the changes in the character of Heathcliff during the course of the novel?

Remember to write about the society he lives in.

Question 6

Great Expectations

Referring to **two** or **three** sections of the novel, show how Dickens creates atmosphere and tension.

Remember to write about the society in which the novel is set.

Question 7

The Withered Arm and Other Wessex Tales

Referring to *The Son's Veto* and one other story, show how Hardy presents attitudes to marriage. Remember to write about the society in which the stories are set.

Question 8

Animal Farm

How effective do you find the ending of *Animal Farm*? Remember to write about the society in which it is set.

Preparation Task

Study the style of the questions above and try to come up with alternative questions on your own text before choosing one and writing a practice answer.

Developing Your Answer

Question 1

Pride and Prejudice

Answer both parts (a) and (b)

Part (a) What impressions do you have of any **two** of the following characters: Lydia Bennet; Mr Bennet; Wickham; Bingley?

Remember to write about the society they live in.

Part (b) How does Austen's way of writing create the characters you have chosen?

This writing frame is designed to give you an idea of the kind of thing you might say and how to organise it. In the exam, you would, of course, expand your points, giving more details and references to the text.

In the time allowed you will not be able to cover every aspect of the question in very great depths, so try to make a few key points quickly and without waffling.

Writing Frame

Part (a)

Name the two characters	Both Elizabeth's father and youngest sister – Mr Bennet and Lydia – have important parts to play in 'Pride and Prejudice'…
What he's like physically and mentally	Mr Bennet is a middle aged, married man. He is described as being…
His situation and the social context	Because he has five daughters and no sons he cannot pass on his property. Therefore, it is important that his daughters marry because at that time they would not have been able to support themselves…
His daughters' feelings about him	All his daughters, especially Elizabeth, love him but he is not very effective as a parent…
Link to Lydia	He certainly has no control over Lydia. She is his youngest daughter. She is described as being…
How she acts and the social context	Lydia shows how foolish and self-centred she is when she gets involved with Mr Wickham. Her elopement would have brought shame on the whole family…
Conclusion, linking the characters	Lydia's actions, and Mr Bennet's lack of action, create problems for the whole family…

Part (b)

How the writer describes them	We learn about both characters from Jane Austen's descriptions of them, which have an ironic tone…
What they say: Lydia	They also show their characters by the way they speak. Lydia talks only about soldiers…
What they say: Mr Bennett	Mr Bennet is witty but has a rather sarcastic way of speaking to his daughters…
Why they are in the novel	Both Lydia and Mr Bennet are useful in showing us aspects of the main characters. When Lydia runs away, Elizabeth thinks Darcy will reject her, but instead he proves how much he loves her…
	We also get ideas of marriage from these characters. We can see from Lydia's marriage that Elizabeth has had a lucky escape…
Conclusion	Jane Austen makes us laugh at these characters and does not develop them in depth or share their thoughts with us, but they are both important to the story…

Developing Your Answer

Question 7

The Withered Arm and Other Wessex Tales

Referring to *The Son's Veto* and one other story, show how Hardy presents attitudes to marriage.

Remember to write about the society in which the stories are set.

Writing Frame

Introduction – second story and brief reasons for comparison	Both 'The Son's Veto' and 'The Withered Arm' include marriages between middle-aged men and much younger women…
Comparison of the relationships – similarity and difference	In both stories the men have had previous relationships and the women have not. However, the past lives of Mr Twycross and Mr Lodge are very different and are treated differently…
Similarity between men's attitudes – Hardy's use of descriptive language	In spite of their differences in characters, the two men both seem to love, or certainly seem to be very attracted to their young wives. Hardy's descriptions of the young women…
Narrative style and focus	Hardy focuses much more on Sophy and Gertrude than on their husbands and we share some of their thoughts and feelings…
Contrast between the two main characters. Gertrude's attitude to marriage	There is, however, a contrast in their attitudes to marriage and their husbands'. Gertrude comes to Wessex as a happy bride and is anxious to keep her husband's love…
Sophy's attitude to marriage	Sophy, on the other hand, is never 'exactly' in love with Twycross and does not seem to think that this matters…
What other characters think of the marriages (setting and society)	There is a contrast between how the marriages are regarded by other characters. We first hear of Lodge's marriage through gossip in the cowshed…
The society they live in, its ideas about marriage and effect of these ideas on the women	In the end, Sophy's marriage is happier than Gertrude's, but both women's stories end in tragedy because of the conventions and ideas of the time they live in…
Conclusion, revisiting the question and considering the evidence	In both stories the women are victims. Marriage itself is not seen as a bad thing or the cause of their tragedies, but Hardy shows that attitudes to marriage at the time…

Preparation Task

If you have studied Hardy's short stories, think about which other stories you could use to answer this question and create your own writing frame before deciding which two stories you would prefer to write about. Then complete the essay.

Approaching Unit 3

Tips for the Controlled Assessment

The unit of study for controlled assessment is called **Unit 3: The Significance of Shakespeare and the English Literary Heritage.**

You will be given one task, which may be divided into two parts (one on Shakespeare and one on texts from the English Literary Heritage):

- You must write about Shakespeare and one other text from the English Literary Heritage (see page 95 for a list of authors).
- You may use one of the texts that the AQA has set for examination in Unit 4, but you do not have to.
- Your text may be prose, poetry or drama. It can even be another Shakespeare play.
- You are allowed clean, unannotated copies of the texts you are writing about.
- You are allowed brief notes.
- You are not allowed to take any other texts, draft essays or detailed plans in with you.
- You are allowed access to a dictionary and thesaurus, and to grammar and spell check programmes.
- You will be given between three and four hours to complete the task under supervision.
- The word limit is 2000 words.

Before the controlled assessment make sure that you:
- Know exactly when and where it will take place.
- Know your texts well. You should read each one several times before the assessment.
- Have chosen the question you are going to answer.

- Thoroughly understand the question.
- Have read the notes you have taken or been given in class and that you understand them.
- Have planned what you are going to write and possibly done a preliminary draft.
- Have kept a record of any sources you have used, for example published notes and websites.
- Have practised writing in the form required.
- Have come up with your own ideas about the texts – the examiner wants to know what you think, not what your teacher thinks.
- Have perfected the PEE technique.

During the controlled assessment make sure that you:
- Are aware of the time: you will be given between three and four hours to complete your work. Be absolutely clear about how long you have and how the time is divided up (it is quite likely it will be spread between three or four one-hour lessons).
- Divide the time well. You may be answering one question or two shorter questions.
- Read your questions carefully to remind yourself of what you are being asked to do.
- Quickly find the texts or sections of texts you will be focusing on. If it helps, annotate them, underlining, highlighting and/or making brief notes.
- Quickly jot down your plan.
- If you have time and think it is useful, do a first draft. Remember that all drafts and plans must be handed in with your completed work.
- Do not ask your teacher or any of your fellow pupils for help.
- Check all your work carefully for errors in spelling, punctuation and grammar.

Final Exam 100%

List of Authors

For Unit 3 and Unit 5 (the two units that lead to controlled assessments) your texts must include work from the English Literary Heritage. The following writers' work may be studied.

Pre-Twentieth Century Poetry

Matthew Arnold
Charlotte Brontë
Robert Browning
Geoffrey Chaucer
Samuel Taylor Coleridge
John Dryden
Thomas Hardy
Robert Herrick
John Keats
Andrew Marvell
Alexander Pope
Percy Bysshe Shelley
Jonathan Swift
William Wordsworth

William Blake
Emily Brontë
Lord Byron
John Clare
John Donne
Oliver Goldsmith
George Herbert
Gerard Manley Hopkins
Christopher Marlowe
John Milton
William Shakespeare
Edmund Spenser
Henry Vaughan
Thomas Wyatt

Twentieth Century Poetry

W.H. Auden
Robert Frost
Ted Hughes
Philip Larkin
Wilfred Owen
Siegfried Sassoon
Dylan Thomas
R.S. Thomas

T.S. Eliot
Seamus Heaney
Elizabeth Jennings
D.H. Lawrence
Sylvia Plath
Stevie Smith
Edward Thomas
W.B. Yeats

Pre-Twentieth Century Prose

Jane Austen
Emily Brontë
Wilkie Collins
Daniel Defoe
George Eliot
Elizabeth Gaskell
Henry James
Robert Louis Stevenson
Anthony Trollope
Oscar Wilde

Charlotte Brontë
John Bunyan
Joseph Conrad
Charles Dickens
Henry Fielding
Thomas Hardy
Mary Shelley
Jonathan Swift
H.G. Wells

Twentieth Century Prose

Kingsley Amis
William Golding
Aldous Huxley
D.H. Lawrence
George Orwell
J.B. Priestley
Stevie Smith
William Trevor
John Wyndham

E.M. Forster
Graham Greene
James Joyce
Katherine Mansfield
Sylvia Plath
Siegfried Sassoon
Muriel Spark
Evelyn Waugh

Pre-Twentieth Century Drama

William Congreve
Oliver Goldsmith
Christopher Marlowe
William Shakespeare
Richard Brinsley Sheridan
Oscar Wilde

Twentieth Century Drama

T.S. Eliot
Sean O'Casey
Harold Pinter
J.B. Priestley
Peter Shaffer
George Bernard Shaw
R.C. Sherriff
Dylan Thomas
Arnold Wesker

Index

A
Alliteration 25, 50
Animal Farm 78–79, 82
Antagonist 18
Apostrophes 7
Aside 67, 69
Assonance 25, 50

C
Character log 20
Characterisation 41, 65
Characters 17–20, 68–69, 80–81
Colons 7
Comedies 73
Commas 7
Conceit 76
Confusing words 7
Connectives 6, 31
Controlled assessment 11, 65
Culture 32

D
Dialogue 25
Diction 49, 76
Dramatic irony 22

E
Epilogue 27
Epiphany 17
Exploring cultures 32–35

F
Fable 84
Facial expressions 19
First person narrative 26, 85
Form 30, 40, 41, 74, 84
Full stops 7

G
Genre 13, 41, 73, 84
Gothic 84
Great Expectations 78–79, 82

H
History and politics 33

I
Iambic pentameter 48, 75
Ideas, themes and issues 14–16, 31, 34, 40, 43
Imagery 51, 76

J
Julius Caesar 72

K
Kindertransport 20, 30

L
Language 23, 24, 33, 34, 38, 85
Literary terms 9–10

M
Macbeth 71, 88
Metaphors 25, 51
Misused words 8
Modern drama 16
Modern prose 14–25
Moon on the Tides 40
Movement 19
Much Ado About Nothing 70–71

N
Narrative 26
Narrator 15

Non-standard English 24

O
Omniscient narrator 85
Onomatopoeia 25, 50
Oxymoron 76

P
Pathetic fallacy 23
PEE 12, 31, 38
Personification 51
Place 23
Poetry 40
Poetry, character and voice 45
Posture 19
Pride and Prejudice 78–79, 81, 82, 92
Protagonist 17
Punctuation 25, 75
Puns 76
Purple Hibiscus 36, 38, 39

Q
Question marks 7
Quotations 12

R
Religion and beliefs 33, 38
Repetition 50
Rhetorical language 76
Rhyme 48, 75
Rhythm 48, 75
Romance 84
Romeo and Juliet 70, 89

S
Satire 84
Semi-colons 7

Settings 21, 82–83
Similes 12, 51, 76
Singh Song 57
Soliloquy 16, 67, 69
Sound 50, 75
Spellbound 56
Stage directions 16
Stage sets 23
Standard English 24
Stanzas 47
Story structure 27
Structure 34, 40
Sunlight on the Grass 13
Syntax 25

T
The Darkness Out There 31
The Prelude 56
The Withered Arm and Other Wessex Tales 78–79, 82, 93
Themes and issues 41, 66–67
Third person narrative 26
Time 21
To Kill a Mockingbird 37
Traditions 33, 39
Tragedies 73
Twelfth Night 72

U
Unseen Poetry 58–63

V
Voice 19, 41

W
Wuthering Heights 78–79, 82

Acknowledgements

Page 20 Quotations from KINDERTRANSPORT copyright © Diane Samuels 1995, 1996, 2008 by permission of the publishers, Nick Hern Books Ltd: www.nickhernbooks.co.uk

Page 36 *Purple Hibiscus* Reprinted by permission of HarperCollins Publishers Ltd © 2003 Chimamanda Ngozi Adichie

Page 37 *To Kill a Mockingbird* by Harper Lee, published by Vintage Classics, £7.99. First published in 1960.

Page 45, *Cold Knap Lake* from *Collected Poems* by Gillian Clarke (Carcanet, 1997). Reprinted by permission of Carcanet Press Limited

Page 45 *The Yellow Palm* from *King Driftwood* by John Minhinnick (Carcanet, 2008). Reprinted by permission of Carcanet Press Limited.

Page 45 Ted Hughes, *Hawk Roosting*, reprinted by permission of Faber and Faber Ltd

Page 46 *The Hunchback in the Park* from *The Poems* by Dylan Thomas. Reproduced by permission of David Higham Associates Limited

Pages 46 and 51 *Quickdraw* from **RAPTURE** by Carol Ann Duffy. Reproduced by permission of Picador, an imprint Pan Macmillian, London. Copyright © Carol Ann Duffy 2005

Page 49 From *Hard Water* by Jean Sprackland, published by Jonathan Cape. Reprinted by permission of The Random House Group Ltd.

Page 49 *Price We Pay for the Sun* from *The Fat Black Woman's Poems* by Grace Nichols. Reproduced by permission of Curtis Brown Group Ltd

Page 49 *Neighbours* from *Collected Poems* by Gillian Clarke (Carcanet, 1997). Reprinted by permission of Carcanet Press Limited

Page 49 *The Manhunt* from *The Not Dead* by Simon Armitage, reproduced by permission of Pomona

Page 49 *Checking Out Me History* by John Agard. Reproduced by permission of Caroline Sheldon Literacy Agency

Pages 49 and 57 Daljit Nagra, *Singh Song*, reprinted by permission of Faber and Faber Ltd

Page 50 Seamus Heaney, *The Blackbird of Glanmore*, reprinted by permission of Faber and Faber Ltd

Page 50 Ted Hughes, *Wind*, reprinted by permission of Faber and Faber Ltd

Page 50 *Crossing the Loch* from **JIZZEN** by Kathleen Jamie. Reproduced by permission of Picador, an imprint Pan Macmillian, London. Copyright © Kathleen Jamie 1999

Page 50 *The Falling Leaves* from *Scars Upon My Heart* by Margaret Postgate Cole. Reproduced by permission of David Higham Associates Limited

Page 51 *Praise Song for My Mother* from *The Fat Black Woman's Poems* by Grace Nichols. Reproduced by permission of Curtis Brown Group Ltd

Page 51 *Below the Green Corrie* from *The Poems of Norman MacCaig* by Norman MacCaig. Reproduced by kind permission of Birlinn Ltd

Page 51 *Nettles* by Vernon Scannell. Reproduced by permission of the Literary Executor for the Estate of Vernon Scannell

Page 63 *Do Not Go Gentle Into That Good Night* from *The Poems* by Dylan Thomas. Reproduced by permission of David Higham Associates Limited

p.2   ©iStockphoto.com / Pamela Cowart-Rickman
p.10   ©iStockphoto.com
p.15   ©iStockphoto.com / Jason van der Valk
p.29   ©iStockphoto.com / Paul-André Belle-Isle
p.32   ©iStockphoto.com
p.40   ©iStockphoto.com / Cole Vineyard
p.51   ©iStockphoto.com / Alex Bramwell
p.65   ©iStockphoto.com / Duncan Walker
p.67   ©iStockphoto.com/Dave White
p.77   ©iStockphoto.com / Duncan Walker
p.89   Stockphoto.com / Christi Tolbert

All other images ©2009 Jupiterimages Corporation and Lonsdale.